MW01602176

the
RESCUE
project

RUNNING RESCUE

for facilitators

REVISED EDITION

Know the Story
Running Rescue *Guide*
Revised Edition
ACTS XXIX, Copyright © 2023. All rights reserved.

Layout by Jacqueline L. Challiss Hill ~ JDetailsLLC.com

Cover Image: ACTS XXIX
Image Credits: 4PM Media

https://rescueproject.us

Synopsis: The Facilitator Guide is a companion resource for The Rescue Project that equips facilitators to lead sessions and small group discussions over the course of eight weeks.

ISBN: 978-1-7364920-7-9
Library of Congress Control Number: 2023903881

Printed in The United States of America

Published by ACTS XXIX Press
38695 Seven Mile Road, Suite 110
Livonia, MI 48152
actsxxix.org | press@actsxxix.org

Table of Contents

Foreword

Section 1: The Essentials

Section 2: Equipping

Section 3: The Rescue Project

FOREWORD

Beauty | Human | Accompaniment

This is a series of reflections on the three words beauty, human and accompaniment that uniquely mark *The Rescue Project*. Most of us appreciate that it's not so much what we do in ministry, but how we do what we do. In a particular way, we believe these three words describe the "how" of *The Rescue Project*.

Beauty
"The world will be saved by beauty."
- Fyodor Dostoevsky

Beauty packs a punch and possesses an evidential power that points to God, the One who is true, good and beautiful. Every person is drawn to beauty. It's transformative.

When we speak about beauty in *The Rescue Project*, we're talking about the beauty of hospitality. Beauty sets the stage for all we do in the eight week experience of the gospel. Everything we do should be beautiful - from the invitations we send, to the tables we set, to the food we present, to the environment we create. Beauty impresses upon a person that we've been expecting them, that they are loved, that they are seen and that they matter. And to be clear, beauty doesn't mean expensive. Sometimes we can wrongly equate the two. We can make things beautiful with a bit of effort, desire and creativity.

A brief story may help illustrate the importance of beauty. We (ACTS XXIX) recently moved into our new office in a secular suburban commercial building. With our suite on the first floor, our hallway sees quite a bit of foot traffic. Through the double glass doors, people can easily see inside. Shortly after our initial weeks in our new place, we overheard a series of conversations in the hallway about our newly decorated space, a space that we have very intentionally created to feel like a home. It's clearly not the typical sterile office you'd expect to see in our complex. We overheard words like "gorgeous" and "beautiful" to describe our new office. Our hope is that these same people who were attracted to the beauty of our office will one day soon be open to an invitation to come and join us for lunch and learn more about our ministry.

You see, beauty attracts. Beauty leaves a lasting impression upon people, whether it's a newly decorated office, our small groups tables, our parish gathering spaces or our homes. Beauty communicates the message that everyone is welcome. And when we experience this caliber of welcome, we are creating opportunities for deeper conversations, conversations that have the potential to change lives. This is why beauty is central in *The Rescue Project*.

Human

"The glory of God is man fully alive." - St. Irenaeus

Perhaps the crisis of our age in both the Church and the world is that we have forgotten what it means to be human. For scores of reasons, many of us feel as though we can't be ourselves out of fear of rejection or that we won't measure up. So we protect ourselves by putting up facades, wearing masks and pretending that we have it all together. This is not living life as God intended. Jesus said, "I came that they may have life, and may have it abundantly (John 10:10)." Unfortunately, many of us don't experience this abundance. In order to be fully alive we need to recapture the essence of what it means to be human.

We contend that what's most needed to recover what it means to be human is to experience love, authentic love. But here's the struggle. To love requires something many of us tend to shy away from - vulnerability. We lose the sense of self-protection when we choose to love and to be loved. C. S. Lewis once said, "To love at all is to be vulnerable."

This is why in *The Rescue Project*, our small groups need to be communities of love where we lean into all manner of being human, making room for joy, sorrow, tears, laughter, excitement and silence. Being human gives others permission to be human. Vulnerability breeds vulnerability. And as we begin to discover the truth of who God is and what He has done for us in His Son, Jesus Christ, we can reclaim our identity as His beloved daughters and sons and live fully human lives, giving glory to God.

Accompaniment

"Next to the Blessed Sacrament itself, your neighbor is the holiest object presented to your senses." C. S. Lewis

Accompaniment is how we walk with others in *The Rescue Project*. As small group facilitators, we take our place among those in the small group and offer ourselves to others as companions on the journey. In Evangelii Gaudium, Pope Francis speaks about accompaniment as an "art," which "teaches us to remove our sandals before the sacred ground of the other (cf. Ex. 3:5). Small groups in *The Rescue Project* are truly holy ground.

Accompanying others as small group leaders requires us to be available, accountable, intentional and vulnerable. One of the most beautiful outcomes of accompanying others in *The Rescue Project* is not only an encounter with Jesus, but also the recovery of what it means to be human and what it means to be a friend.

Accompaniment in *The Rescue Project* moves beyond the typical sporadic encounters we sometimes have with others by pressing into a regular rhythm over eight weeks, with intentional touchpoints in between sessions if needed or desired. Over time, walking with those in our small group allows for a progressive unveiling of who God is, a deeper understanding of our identity and the plan He has for our lives. Being attentive and docile to the Holy Spirit, leading with joy, asking great questions and listening with the same passion with which you want to be heard are essential components when walking with others. As friendships begin to form, we're able to move from simply engaging on the natural level to an engagement of the heart, allowing for vulnerability, sharing our own insights and our own stories when prompted by the Holy Spirit.

As you move through the journey, you will discover that walking with others isn't a linear process. As Abigail Favale writes, "Conversion is a steady pilgrimage, a long trek into the heart of God. There are detours and switchbacks along the way; none of us hike straight; none of us can manage alone. Accompaniment evokes this sense of conversion over time, as well as the need for community along the way." Over time you may be invited to go deeper in a particular area that the other is allowing you to speak into.

In our zeal and our passion for the gospel, it's important when walking with others in the small group to keep in mind that this is their journey and to remind ourselves not to get ahead of them by offering answers to questions that aren't being asked. It's necessary to understand that what's most needed at times is the gift of our presence and an attentive ear.

There is no greater joy than walking with another to help bring them into a deeper friendship with Jesus. Loving as Jesus does and pressing into our own relationship with Jesus makes such accompaniment possible.

WHAT IS *THE RESCUE PROJECT*?

The Rescue Project seeks to proclaim the gospel in a compelling and attractive way over eight weeks in a small group format. The goal of *The Rescue Project* is to create an opportunity for people to be overwhelmed and be brought to a decision to surrender their lives to Jesus and be mobilized for mission.

The Rescue Project is intended for use anywhere—in parish ministries such as RCIA, sacramental preparation, evangelization, discipleship, men's groups, women's groups, youth ministry, and more. It's also easily run in homes, restaurants, workplaces, schools, and prisons. It appeals to those who have been walking with Jesus for years, as well as those for whom Jesus is only a figure in ancient history. In other words, *The Rescue Project* is for everyone, everywhere, whether inside or outside of the Church.

OUR APOSTOLIC VALUES

ACTS XXIX has three apostolic core values that deeply influence and guide our mission, as well as inform the culture of *The Rescue Project*. ACTS XXIX's apostolic core values are: 1) Ambitious for God and His Kingdom;

2) Authentically Human; and 3) Docile to the Holy Spirit. Everyone involved in *The Rescue Project* will encounter these values imbued in every facet of the experience.

Ambitious for God and His Kingdom

When we plan, prepare, and equip to run *The Rescue Project*, we want to lead with an ambitiousness for God and His Kingdom. What does that mean? It means we are convicted that God has set us apart for this work and is doing something bigger than us. It also means that we have unshakable confidence in the Lordship of Jesus, that we are His witnesses and not experts, and that He wants to use us to help get His world back.

Authentically Human

We have an authentically human approach to mission. By that we mean we promise to help each other lead a balanced life. It means we give each other permission to be real, acknowledging that it's okay not to be okay and we seek to be of one heart and one mind, all for the sake of mission. It also means that we make intentional time to enjoy each other's company. *The Rescue Project* small group uniquely allows for this honest and human approach to friendship and conversation.

Docile to the Holy Spirit

Docility to the Holy Spirit means that we pray in order to know what to do, restoring the initiative to God. This necessarily implies that we have a willingness to go wherever He leads, leaving the familiar behind. It also means that rather than rowing in a rowboat, growing weary from our efforts, we sail as in a sailboat, allowing His Spirit to move the sails forward in the manner and direction He desires to lead us. Prayer is the lifeblood of *The Rescue Project*, informing how we plan, prepare, equip, and promote as well as how we lead and care for those in our small groups.

RESOURCES

All the resources you need to run *The Rescue Project* are available online at https://rescueproject.us.

They include nine videos, The Story Guide, equipping videos, and all the companion resources for facilitators and administrators. We also have downloadable assets to help promote your *Rescue Project*.

ESSENTIAL ELEMENTS

● Prayer ● Meal ● Worship
● Episode ● Conversation

THE WEEKLY SESSION

The Rescue Project may be offered over any meal on any day of the week. The general run time is roughly 2 hours.

Here is a sample schedule of a Rescue evening:

5:30 p.m. **Pre-session Rescue huddle for facilitators (20-30 min.)*

6:00 p.m. People arrive and are seated in their small groups

6:05 p.m. The session begins with welcome, prayer, and an overview of the evening

6:10 p.m. Dinner

6:55 p.m. Worship music

7:00 p.m. *Rescue Project* episode

7:45 p.m. Small group conversation

8:15 p.m. Session concludes

8:20 p.m. ***Post-session Rescue huddle with facilitators (10 min.)*

* The pre-session Rescue huddle allows for time to gather together with the table facilitators and the session leader (if applicable for your context) to review what the upcoming session will look like, answer any questions and pray together for the session ahead.
** The post-session Rescue huddle allows for time to debrief the small group experience and to discuss what went well, what didn't, and what you may need to be attentive to moving forward.

THE RETREAT

The Rescue Project retreat creates an opportunity for participants to respond to all God has done for them and to surrender their lives to Jesus in faith. Designed to be offered in half a day, roughly 8 am to 1:30 pm, the retreat is offered easily in a parish or a home.

The content of the retreat consists of two videos - Episode 7: Words are Not Enough and Episode 8: What Does He Want from Me? The day also includes worship, prayerful reflection, small group discussion and an opportunity to receive prayer ministry. If the retreat is offered in a parish setting, the retreat may either begin or conclude with Mass.

As you prepare for the retreat, we offer this checklist to assist with your planning.

A sample schedule may look something like this:

7:15 a.m.	Mass
8:00 a.m.	Welcome, orientation, prayer
8:10 a.m.	Breakfast
8:55 a.m.	Worship
9:10 a.m.	*Rescue Project* Chapter Seven: Words Are Not Enough
9:55 a.m.	Journaling and prayerful reflection
10:25 a.m.	Break
10:45 a.m.	*Rescue Project* Chapter Eight: What Does He Want From Me?

11:30 a.m.	Communal Surrender Prayer
11:45 a.m.	Prayer Ministry *(take as long as you need)*
12:45 p.m.	Lunch
1:30 p.m.	Debrief ("What did the Lord do?")
2:00 p.m.	Worship, prayer, conclude

Retreat Checklist

For larger retreats in a parish context, you may want to consider creating a retreat planning team to oversee the details. For smaller retreats in the home, adapt accordingly.

✔ Identify the date, time frame and venue for the retreat.
✔ Remind small group leaders to continue to message, invite and encourage people to attend.
✔ Plan worship by recruiting a worship leader or create a worship playlist.
✔ Schedule a prayer ministry refresher training for small group leaders by watching the equipping video on prayer ministry.
✔ Plan the meals, hospitality and welcome.
  • Screens
  • Projectors
  • Mics
  • Flat screen TV
✔ Arrange for childcare if needed
✔ Create an intercessory prayer team that will cover the day in prayer.
✔ Build a schedule for guests.
✔ Encourage participants to bring a journal and/or The Story Guide.

✔ Invite small group leaders to spiritually prepare for prayer ministry by encouraging them to visit the Sacrament of Reconciliation prior to the retreat.

✔ Write thank you notes to all who made the retreat possible.

What Is the Purpose of the Retreat?

What is the purpose of the retreat, and especially the purpose of praying with those who are going through *The Rescue Project?*

As the title of Chapter 7 says, "Words are not enough." Something more than just hearing what Jesus has done for us by His Death and Resurrection needs to happen. Someone needs to happen. That someone is the Holy Spirit.

What exactly, then, are we praying for?

Well, for those who are not yet baptized, we're praying that the Holy Spirit will come upon them and enable them to know that this is true! That the One through whom the universe was made became man for them! That out of love God has come, in disguise, to fight for them, to liberate them from the tyranny of Death and Sin and hell. God wants to do this more than we want it to happen, and so we can pray with great confidence. Jesus said, "If you, then, who are wicked, know how to give good gifts to your children, how much more will the Father in heaven give the Holy Spirit to those who ask Him?" (Luke 11:13).

Hopefully, for those who are not yet baptized, going through *The Rescue Project* will create in them a desire to receive the sacrament of baptism and to come into the Church, where they can receive all that God desires to give them so that their "joy may be full" (John 15:11).

What about those who have already been baptized? For what are we praying on the retreat?

Cardinal Cantalamessa writes, "For many Christians, Baptism is a bound sacrament [ineffective because of some obstacle] ... because of the lack of personal faith which confirms and accepts the sacrament. It's similar to a great gift-box that we received at the moment of our re-birth in God, a gift-box that has never been opened but has been left there unopened, through indifference. We are rich because we possess the 'titles' of children of God, heirs of Jesus Christ, members of the Mystical Body, temples of the Holy Spirit, and we can legitimately carry out all the practices of Christian life but we don't know that we are rich and not knowing it, we don't use this wealth but live poorly" (Life in the Lordship of Christ, vii).

Perhaps more simply, we could say the purpose of our praying with those who have already been baptized on the retreat is that the Holy Spirit will "renew" and "actualize" in them what they already received in the sacrament of baptism, to help those who come forward to know – to experience in their concrete lives – the life-changing reality that Jesus is Lord!

Of course, the Holy Spirit might manifest Himself in many other ways as well, and often does. But those things are secondary to this gift, this grace from God: knowing that Jesus is Lord, and that there is no other; that all we have spoken about thus far is true; and that the proper response to what He has done is surrender. This is what faith is.

(For further reading, see Sober Intoxication of the Spirit: Born Again of Water and the Spirit: Part Two, Raniero Cardinal Cantalamessa, Servant Books, 2012).

ROLES AND TEAMS

● Coordinator ● Session Leader
● Small Group Facilitators ● Hospitality Team
● Worship Team ● Prayer Team

COORDINATOR

The coordinator serves as the touch point for *The Rescue Project*, and is responsible for overseeing every aspect of running *The Rescue Project* in any context, including planning, promoting, and administrating the project. This person also oversees equipping, forming key teams, and securing feedback. The ideal coordinator is someone who is passionate for the gospel, possesses pastoral gifts, enjoys administration, and is organized.

SESSION LEADER

The session leader serves as somewhat of an emcee, oversees the weekly sessions, welcomes everyone, and offers an overview of each session. This person is also the time-keeper, making sure every session runs smoothly and begins and ends on time. The ideal session leader is someone who is organized, warm, engaging, and personable. The session leader will be the primary contact for table facilitators and will lead the pre- and post-session huddles. The emcee role requires this person to be comfortable up front as the focal point for each session.

What does this role look like?

1. Prior to the pre-session huddle:
   - Check all A/V equipment to make sure technology is working.
   - You may wish to download the episodes to avoid connectivity issues.
   - Select one or two worship songs and make sure they are queued up to play.
   - Make sure the facilitators are at the table and ready to receive everyone when they arrive.
   - Make sure the meal is prepared and ready to be served.

2. Thirty minutes prior to the start of a session, gather your facilitators to:
   - Welcome them.
   - Give leaders an opportunity to introduce themselves in the event they don't already know one another.

- Answer any questions they may have.
- Briefly introduce the session topic.
- Address any concerns from the prior session.
- Lead the group in worship and prayer.
- Dismiss them in time for them to greet their small groups.

3. At the start of the session:
   - Begin on time.
   - Welcome everyone.
   - Introduce yourself.
   - Announce the menu and begin the meal.
   - Invite the small group leaders to bless the meal at their tables.
   - Keep track of the time.
   - Five minutes before the end of the meal, politely give a five-minute "warning" to everyone, announcing that the next segment of the session will begin.
   - Play a worship song or two, inviting everyone who feels comfortable to join in.
   - Begin the *Rescue* episode after worship.
   - Allow everyone a five-minute break after the episode.
   - Announce the beginning of small group discussion.
   - Watch the time. Group discussion should last roughly thirty minutes. Offer a five-minute warning before the end of the session.
   - End promptly, though some people may linger.
   - Encourage the facilitators to complete the feedback.

4. Between each session:
   - Pray for your group.
   - Remind your table facilitators to pray for their small group.
   - Remind them of the retreat date.
   - Encourage them to email or contact you if there are questions or concerns about their small group.
   - Be a source of love, encouragement and prayer for your leaders.

SMALL GROUP FACILITATORS

Small group leaders are facilitators of conversation who encourage balanced discussion among everyone in the group. The small group facilitator prays for, loves, accompanies, and serves those in their group. The ideal facilitator is a companion on the journey who is prayerful, attentive to the Holy Spirit, joyful, relational and has a heart for mission and for others.

HOSPITALITY TEAM

This team is responsible for creating an atmosphere of welcome and beauty. A wise woman once remarked that everything we do in ministry should be beautiful. We couldn't agree more. Beauty attracts and first impressions are never forgotten.

The purpose of the hospitality team is to impress upon each person that they are loved, seen, and that they matter, making sure every participant is greeted warmly before they arrive to their small group.

The hospitality team is composed of a number of people who may serve in a variety of capacities. They greet people as they arrive, serve the meal, and decorate the space in such a way that people are overwhelmed when they walk into the room. The ideal hospitality team member is creative, energetic, and enjoys serving others.

MEAL TEAM

This team oversees how meals will be offered during *The Rescue Project*. The meal is truly the ultimate ice-breaker and is the place where real conversations happen. Meals may be catered or prepared onsite. Meals may also be offered pot-luck style, creating an opportunity to get everyone involved in making the meal special. Get creative to make the meals great and affordable. The ideal meal team member appreciates the importance of food and loves serving others.

WORSHIP TEAM

This team oversees the integration of worship music weekly in *The Rescue Project*. Worship is an integral element in the experience. Worship breaks open the heart so the Word of God may be planted within. Worship music may be live or played on a device by accessing Spotify, Amazon Music, or iTunes. This team also coordinates worship for the retreat. The ideal worship team member appreciates the role of beautiful music as a means to help facilitate an encounter with God.

INTERCESSORY PRAYER TEAM

This team prays for everyone involved in *The Rescue Project*, including leaders, participants, and planners. This team secures a list from the coordinator of everyone involved in *The Rescue Project* and prays for them by name throughout the eight weeks. The ideal person for this team is someone who possesses the gift of intercessory prayer.

OTHER CONTEXTS
Outside the Parish

The Rescue Project may be offered in a variety of contexts outside the parish. For instance, it may be offered in homes, workplaces, schools, local restaurants, or prisons. In these environments, you might very well serve in every role with the exception of the co-facilitator as these are generally smaller groups.

In some of the contexts, it may not be feasible to offer worship music. What is important is to maintain these key ingredients: prayer, the meal, the episode, and the small group discussion.

The retreat component of *The Rescue Project* may be navigated in these contexts by getting creative about how best to gather, watch two episodes, allow for your small group to respond, surrender, and be prayed with should they be open to receiving prayer ministry.

EQUIPPING

TOPIC 1: SMALL GROUPS

The equipping offered in this guide is not intended to be exhaustive, but rather to complement the Running Rescue online equipping videos online. https://rescueproject.us

The intention for this topic is to offer you some practical tips for facilitating healthy and balanced conversation in *The Rescue Project* small group.

Goals

The purpose of *The Rescue Project* small group is to create a safe space for authentic conversations with the hope that meaningful friendships with one another and with God will be established.

Jesus didn't make disciples in a classroom. He did it by doing life together. *The Rescue Project* small group is all about relationships. C. S. Lewis said, "The best place to support friendship is in a small circle of friends." We couldn't agree more. In *The Rescue Project* small group, our aim is to share not only our insights, thoughts, and reflections, but also our very lives (cf 1 Thessalonians 2:8).

Size and Composition

The ideal size of a *Rescue Project* small group is eight participants, one facilitator, and one co-facilitator for a total of ten people. It's worth keeping in mind that if the small group is too large, some people may have the experience of not being seen and heard. Conversely, if the group is too small, the conversation dynamic may become challenging and present too much pressure to talk.

Small groups may be comprised of only men, only women, or a blend of both. The groups may be a mix of all ages or grouped according to seasons of life, interests, and friendships. An important thought to keep in mind is to balance the number of men and women in mixed groups.

Role of the Facilitator and Co-Facilitator

Each Rescue Project small group has two facilitators. The wisdom of having two leaders is quite simple–it's Biblical. Just as no one is meant to do life alone, no one is meant to lead alone. When leading in pairs, one never uses the word, "I"; it's always "we." While the roles of the facilitators may look a bit different, both are needed to run a healthy and engaging small group.

Keep in mind, *Rescue Project* small group leaders are not intended to be teachers, but rather facilitators of conversation in order to encourage balanced discussion among everyone in the group. In other words, small group leaders understand they don't need to have all the answers. That's a relief, right? In *The Rescue Project*, small group leaders are people who are prayerful and attentive to the movement of the Holy Spirit. Additionally, they are joyful, attentive listeners, and have a heart for Jesus, the Church, and the lost. The easiest way to describe a facilitator is a friend on the journey.

The lead facilitator's responsibilities include welcoming everyone to the small group and ensuring appropriate introductions are made. They open with prayer, begin and guide the discussion, bring clarity and direction to the conversation when needed, and invite everyone's participation, paying particular attention to dominating personalities and those who are more quiet and reserved.

The co-facilitator's primary responsibility is one of service and includes helping with hospitality, making sure the group has everything they need, and supporting discussion when necessary. Additionally, the co-facilitator serves as a prayer intercessor for the group discussion, quietly interceding for the conversation. The co-facilitator is also attentive to every person during the meal and an observer of body language, anticipating and meeting unspoken needs of group members. They may also be needed to lead small group conversations in the event the lead facilitator is unable to be present.

Rescue Project facilitators should also attend the pre-session huddle to prayerfully prepare for the session and the post-session debrief to unpack the small group experience.

TIPS FOR FACILITATING

Friends, keep in mind, perfection is not required to lead a *Rescue Project* small group. If that were the case, none of us would step into the role! What is important is leading with prayer, welcoming people with love, being authentically who you are, asking great open-ended questions and being an "in-their- shoes" attentive listener.

These are some simple reminders to keep in mind as you guide your small group. It's not exhaustive by any means, but we think you'll find these basics helpful.

The DOs and DON'Ts | Small Groups

Please DO...

✔ Adopt a mission-minded approach to your small group.

✔ Be attentive to the Holy Spirit and remember it is His job, through you, to reveal the love of Jesus to your small group.

✔ Pray throughout the week for your small group members by name.

✔ Affirm every person and their contribution to the small group, even if you may not agree with their position.

✔ Greet people by name.

✔ Model humility.

✔ Show mutual respect for everyone and their opinions.

✔ Cultivate a safe and comfortable environment.

✔ Maintain confidentiality in the group.

✔ Respect people's busy lives by beginning and ending on time.

✔ Be attentive to the person who seems to be

engaged the least and make every effort to make him or her feel safe, cared for, and loved.

✔ Encourage everyone to ask questions. Remember, there's no such thing as a dumb question.

✔ Make eye-contact with others, showing interest in what they are saying.

✔ Be comfortable with silence.

✔ Create space for everyone to speak, allowing equal time to each person.

✔ Be yourself, enjoy, and have fun.

✔ Allow time at the end of the small group to debrief with your co-facilitator.

Please DON'T...

● Pressure anyone to speak, pray, or directly ask them to participate.

● Speak more than those in your small group. In fact, a helpful gauge at the end of the small group time is to reflect on how much you spoke.

● Interrupt others.

● Ask people if they're Catholic. More often than not, a person's faith affiliation will become evident as discussion continues.

- Allow tangents. The small group discussion should be focused on the content and the questions, and not drift towards personal problems.

- Allow one or two people to dominate the small group, even if unintentionally. Redirect and rephrase questions when necessary.

- Allow people to interrupt one another. Only one person should talk at a time. In other words, discourage side discussions and talking over each other.

- Engage in arguments. Love always wins the day.

Ice Breakers

Ice breakers are fun and create a way to begin building community and friendship in the first couple weeks.

Here are a few, should you want to use them:

- Have each person share something that makes him or her unique or unusual, such as "I've never left the state I was born in" or "I am one of 10 kids."

- "Your house is on fire, and everyone is safe. You have 30 seconds to run through the house and collect three or four articles you want to save. What would you grab? Why?"

❄ Ask each person to name three people, past or present, he or she admires. Why?

❄ Ask, "If you could interview anyone in history, who would you choose and why? What one or two questions would you ask?"

❄ What do you do for fun?

❄ What would be your ideal vacation? What is the most memorable activity you did with your family as a child?

❄ What quality do you appreciate most in a friend?

❄ What is one characteristic you received from your parents you want to keep and one you wish you could change?

❄ Name one good thing happening in your life right now? What makes it good?

NAVIGATING DISCUSSIONS

Small group facilitators may from time to time encounter some challenging dynamics. It's worthwhile to anticipate how to maneuver a few temperaments you may encounter along the way.

The Talkative Person

Dominant personalities are great to get the conversation going, but can also easily derail the small group. Here are a few simple suggestions that may help get discussion back on track:

- Redirect the question to others in your group by asking, "Let's hear from some of you who haven't had a chance to share yet."

- Sit next to the person so as to minimize eye contact. This subtle strategy works.

- It may be helpful to approach this person after the small group and invite them to help you draw others into the conversation by being comfortable with silence so as to allow others to speak.

The Quiet Person

A wise man once said, "Still waters run deep." Simply because someone is quiet doesn't mean they don't have something to say. Often they will speak in due time. Quiet people may simply need time to process their thoughts. Here are a few suggestions that may help to get them engaged:

- While we discourage directly calling on anyone, you may from time to time prayerfully consider asking something as simple as, "What are you thinking and feeling right now?"

- Sit across from them in order to maintain good eye contact. Communicating with body language is immensely helpful.

- Offer positive feedback when they do speak so as to encourage further sharing.

TOPIC 2: PRAYER MINISTRY

This chapter intends to equip you to pray for your *Rescue Project* small group on the retreat. The retreat is the capstone of *The Rescue Project*.

Goals

The purpose of prayer ministry is to facilitate an encounter with the Holy Spirit and to create an opportunity for people to surrender their lives to Jesus by faith.

But first, a word on prayer. Prayer is the foundation of *The Rescue Project*. Everything we do in the project begins and ends with prayer throughout the weekly experience.

By virtue of our baptism, we are priests, and, as Abbot Jeremy Driscoll says, "It's the priest's work to bring another before God in prayer." That's the simplest definition of prayer ministry–we're bringing people before God in prayer, whether we're praying at the beginning or end of our small groups or on the retreat.

On the retreat, the small group facilitators move into praying with and for their small group individually for an outpouring of the Holy Spirit to be convinced that all that God has done is for them, personally, by name and to surrender to Jesus. While everyone is invited to receive prayer ministry, no one should be forced or compelled to receive it.

Preparing for Prayer Ministry

● Prior to prayer ministry on the retreat, prepare spiritually by going to the Sacrament of Reconciliation if you're able.

● Before the retreat, gather together and pray with your facilitator/co-facilitator, inviting the Holy Spirit to be present, with a particular attentiveness to what He may be saying.

● Ask for the grace of docility to the Holy Spirit and to recognize wisdom and words of knowledge.

Prayer Ministry: A Walkthrough

WARM WELCOME

1. **Introduce yourself & the intercessor**
   "Hello, my name is _____ and this is _____, what is your name?"
   "It's great to meet you _____"

2. **Ask if they have received prayer ministry before**
   "Have you ever experienced prayer ministry before?"
   • Honor the answer (yes or no), then...

ORIENT

1. **Explain the prayer ministry process.**
   · Walk them through what they can expect; sharing that they don't need to do anything, but receive
   · Ask them to simply be attentive to what they may be experiencing during prayer
   "What we are going to do right now, is pray for an outpouring of the Holy Spirit. Is that good with you?" (wait for response)
   · The prayee might ask for something else, if they do, receive it and let them know you will pray for that as well

2. **Invite them to a posture that is comfortable for them to pray; our recommendation is to stand with hands open. Ask if you can lay your hand on their shoulder.**

PRAY

1. **Sign of the cross.**

2. **Pray of thanksgiving to the Father for the gift of this person (honors him/her):**
   "Thank you, Father, for gift of (insert name) and for his/her willingness to come forward to pray. Father, we know it's your desire to make yourself known to us, to Father us, bless us, and to bring each to true freedom and happiness through your Son, Jesus."
   · If they are well known to you, feel free to get more specific about them in your gratitude to God for their life.

3. **Pray to Jesus thanking Him for who He is, what He has done for us.**

   "Jesus, we thank you, for rescuing each of us from Sin, Death, and Hell. Lord, thank you for revealing the Father to us, and for inviting us to be your friend."

   · If they have brought up an intention, you can use the following prayer:

   "Jesus, in a particular way right now, we ask you to hear the intentions _____(insert name) has brought forward. Specifically, we pray for (name intentions) _____ (bless _____, heal _____, etc.) and anything else that only you know they need."

   for 3:4

4. **Pray to the Holy Spirit asking for an outpouring.**

   "Holy Spirit, we now ask you to come. Come in your love, come in your power, come in your mercy, come in your peace, and fill _____ (insert name). Come Holy Spirit, unleash your power within _____ (insert name). Holy Spirit, you are the giver of all good gifts, give your son/daughter all the gifts you want him/her to have. Move in his/her heart, move in his/her life. Help him/her to know they are loved, just as they are. Come Holy Spirit, come..."

   · Pause... wait... listen... respond as you are led.

   · Check in, and ask:

   "What are you experiencing right now?"

   · Pause, wait, watch... respond

   · Encourage them and close the prayer

   Active
   Love
   Listen
   to HolySpirit.7

   Com
   Jesus Holy Spirit Accompment
   Holy Ffse Ct 16i1

5. **Closing prayer to end ministry.**

   "Father, thank you for this opportunity to pray with your son/daughter _____ (insert name). Jesus thank you for the graces of this moment, please protect _____ (insert name) from all attacks of the enemy. And Holy Spirit, I pray that you would continue to minister to him/her in the days ahead and continue to transform them into the person God desires them to be. Amen."

After Prayer Ministry

Together with your prayer partner, give God the glory for all He did in this ministry time.

Next are some simple reminders to keep in mind as you lead prayer ministry. It's not exhaustive by any means, but we think you'll find these basics helpful.

The DOs and DON'Ts | Prayer Ministry

Please DO...

✔ Designate a prayer space and have tissues or chairs available should they be necessary.

✔ Minister in pairs, with one lead and one intercessor, working together.

✔ Introduce yourself as a team and ask if the person receiving prayer has received prayer ministry before. If the answer is no, explain what the ministry will look like.

✔ Encourage the person to receive and to relax, opening their hands in a posture of receptivity.

✔ Be warm, friendly, and encouraging.

✔ Respect the person who's coming for prayer.

✔ Lead with love.

✔ Use the gift of tongues with sensitivity, praying quietly.

✔ Avoid theatrics and/or eccentric behavior. In other words, use common and simple language.

✔ Be attentive to what the Holy Spirit is doing, trusting in God.

✔ Always ask if you can place your hand on someone's shoulder before you do so.

✔ Always assure the individual of the Father's love for them.

✔ Maintain confidentiality.

✔ Have mints on hand to keep your breath fresh.

Please DON'T...

● Lay hands on someone without their permission and/or make the laying on of hands uncomfortable or distracting.

● Assume it's all up to you.

● Assume God isn't using you.

● Offer counseling or give advice for life situations.

● Rebuke, correct, or offer your personal opinions or interpretations.

● Pray in tongues in a manner that is distracting.

● Assume every word that comes to mind is of God.

worldview

Chapter One

The Importance of Stories

"This is how stories work. They invite listeners into a new world and encourage them to make it their own, to see their ordinary world from now on through this lens, within this grid." [1]

- N.T. Wright,
Jesus and the Victory of God

THEMES

The Four Big Questions

• Why is there something, rather than nothing?
• Why is everything so messed up?
• What, if anything, has God done about it?
• And if he's done anything, how should I respond?

QUESTIONS TO CONSIDER

• What is the story that gives me meaning, purpose, and guides my life?
• What is my image of God?
• Where did that image of God come from?

_____

_____

_____

_____

_____

_____

_____

_____

_____

_____

_____

_____

_____

_____

_____

_____

_____

_____

_____

_____

_____

Facilitator Resources

Chapter Summary

We are all shaped by stories. The choices we make, the way we live, the things we believe—the way we see life itself—are all the result of the stories that we have embraced as truthful accounts of reality. Our modern world, for example, presents the story that we are personally liberated, no longer connected to anything beyond ourselves, and free to do whatever we like. And we, it would seem, have never been more restless or unhappy.

In light of this, The Rescue Project proposes a question: what if the story is different? What if we were created by an all-loving God in His image for friendship, communion, and love? What if we foolishly rebelled against the Creator and allowed ourselves to be captured by an enemy seeking to destroy us? What if we were then rescued by the Son of God Himself who went to war on our behalf against Sin, Death, and Hell? And what if we were called to respond to that act of God's supreme love both as a race and as individuals?

What would that look like?

GOALS

- Identify "the lenses" through which we see reality.
- Realize how a Biblical view of existence might change those perceptions.

Chapter Topics

- The Role of Stories in Our Lives
- The State of Contemporary Culture
- The Four Big Questions of the Christian Life
- The Biblical Definition of the Gospel

ACTION ITEMS

- Focus in these early stages on setting a comfortable atmosphere for your group. Remember, keep the initial conversations light, listen as much as you can, and don't be afraid to laugh a little.
- Be prepared to step in and gently direct the conversation if one or two participants seem to dominate. Try to move the discussion around by

asking what others think about the topic. Not everyone will want to contribute early on so don't worry if certain individuals are more reluctant to talk than others.

PASTORAL NOTES

1. Meeting participants where they are.
People come to *The Rescue Project* for all kinds of different reasons. Some, for example, seek out the experience on their own while others are brought by a friend or family member. As a result, there will likely be a range of reactions to the material and concepts. Be aware of each participant's comfort level and do your best to meet them where they are.

2. Helping participants recognize "their story."
Not everyone will recognize that they might see the world through a particular set of lenses. This is an opportunity to explore in some general (and non-judgmental) ways the things that are most important to the individuals in your group. Some of us view life primarily in relation to our careers or our families or our politics. Try to keep the discussion light and perhaps even frame it as a starting point for further, deeper reflection.

QUESTIONS TO CONSIDER

What is the story that gives you meaning, purpose, and guides your life?
Be attentive to the way that people introduce themselves to the rest of the group. Oftentimes, this can offer insight into the story that defines a particular person's view of the world. If a participant is having difficulty answering this question, remind them that they mentioned being a mom or that they worked for a certain company when sharing about themselves and ask (gently!) how much that aspect of their personality defines who they are.

What is your image of God?
Many participants will likely reach for one of the more common, affirmative conceptions of God: a loving father-figure, a spiritual judge, or perhaps even a good friend. Be ready, however, for negative impressions—angry, condemning, absentee—and remember that it isn't your responsibility to engage in a debate or change anyone's mind. Trust the Holy Spirit—and the material—and allow the conversation with your group proceed without feeling the need to steer participants down particular pathways.

Where did that image of God come from?
The response to this question can be tremendously illuminating. Answers will typically range from reading

Scripture to what individuals learned in religion classes. Those experiences can be both good and bad, of course, depending on the individual. Understand that some have been poorly catechized or have experienced trauma that can shape their impression, too. Also, we often project onto God our experiences with parents, caretakers, and authority figures. Be prepared to discuss all of these possibilities.

DEEPER QUESTIONS

[This section is designed to help facilitators reflect on key questions as a way of preparing for the full range of issues addressed—both directly and indirectly—by this session. These questions might also be used with participants who seem ready or eager to take the discussion beyond the topics dealt with in the Questions to Consider section of the Participant's Guide.]

1. Have you, yourself, ever been overwhelmed by the message of the gospel?

_____

_____

_____

_____

2. What are the most significant impediments to living a Christian life in our contemporary world?

_____

_____

_____

_____

_____

_____

_____

3. To what degree has your faith evolved over the course of your life?

_____

_____

_____

_____

_____

_____

_____

SUGGESTED READING

Sophia Consulting. *Christian Cosmic Narrative: The Deep History of the World,* 2021.

Riccardo, Fr. John. *Rescued: The Unexpected and Extraordinary News of the Gospel,* 2020.

---

1. Wright, *Jesus and the Victory of God,* 176.

Chapter Two

Why Is There Something Rather than Nothing?

"Either all individual things are the product of evolution, including man, or else they are not... Of course, the question remains open whether being ... has a meaning and it cannot be decided within the theory of evolution itself; for that theory this is a methodologically foreign question, although of course for a live human being it is the fundamental question on which the whole thing depends." [2]

- Joseph Ratzinger,
Credo for Today: What Christians Believe

THE GRACE: *Wonder and Awe*

And God made the two great lights, the greater light to rule the day and the lesser light to rule the night; he made the stars also.[3]

Genesis 1:16

THEMES

The Biblical Story

- There is one God.
- He is good.
- He creates out of love (and not need).
- He creates effortlessly.
- The human person is the highlight of everything that he creates.
- We are made in his image and likeness.
- We are made for friendship, love, and communion with God and with each other.

QUESTIONS TO CONSIDER

- How does pondering the grandeur of creation instill a sense of wonder and awe in my life? How or why?
- Is my image of God changing? Yes or No? Explain.
- What's causing me anxiety right now? How does the God of the biblical story impact that?

_____

_____

_____

_____

_____

_____

_____

_____

_____

_____

Facilitator Resources

Chapter Summary

Chapter Two begins our exploration of the Biblical Story by asking the question, "Why is there something rather than nothing?" The answer offered by the Catholic Church is simple: because the universe was formed effortlessly by God out of love for a creature made in His image and likeness. That creature is you and me, and we were created for friendship, communion, and love, first with God and then with each other.

GOALS

- Understand God's original plan for creation.
- Recognize how Genesis reveals God's true relationship with the human race and with each of us individually.

Chapter Topics

- The Goodness of Creation
- Genesis Chapters 1-3 as Inspired Poetry
- The Uniqueness of Genesis in Ancient World Literature
- The Grandeur of the Universe
- Humanity as the Highlight of Creation

ACTION ITEMS

- Begin to take note of participant reactions to the content (positive or negative) in order to better tend to individual needs throughout *The Rescue Project* experience.
- Prepare participants for the fact that Sessions 3 and 4 are going to be hard, but assure them that the news is ultimately good. Knowledge is power!
- Offer to make yourself available for coffee or a phone call or a conversation by email with participants who might have additional questions or feel the need to follow up with any of the content.

PASTORAL NOTES

1. Participants' preconceived notions of God

Understand that participants will bring to *The Rescue Project* a range of views about God, including those that arise from trauma and pain earlier in their lives. Again, be careful also not to presume that everyone is ready to embrace the idea of God as a Good Father, even after watching the session. Try to assess where each of your participants is individually, be sensitive to that position, and meet them where they are.

2. How to read Scripture

Many participants will come to *The Rescue Project*, whether by formation or habit, assuming that the Bible, as a whole, is intended to be read literally and that the content of Genesis, specifically, is to be taken as history and/or science. The Catholic Church teaches that the Bible, rather than a single unified "book," is actually more like a library or a collection of texts consisting of many genre (literary types), including biography, history, prophecy, poetry, law, and allegory. Just as we read a newspaper article with different expectations than we might a science fiction novel, so we approach one book of the Bible differently than we might another. Please encourage participants to read "Dogmatic Constitution of Divine Revelation" in the resources section at the end of Chapter 2 for a fuller discussion of Biblical genres and approaches to interpretation.

3. Graphic nature of ANE myths

A brief warning that most Ancient Near East creation stories contain excessive violence and graphic sexual content. There are many other examples beyond the two that are discussed briefly in this session. The point of mentioning them, again, is to illustrate the absolute uniqueness of the creation account in Genesis 1 and 2 compared to those of ancient Israel's neighbors.

QUESTIONS TO CONSIDER

How does pondering the grandeur of creation instill a sense of wonder and awe in your life?

Many of us, it seems, are so wrapped up in the things that inform our daily lives (our responsibilities, our anxieties, our expectations) that we fail to appreciate the often-indescribable magnificence of the natural world all around us—everything from the beauty of a single small flower to the splendor of the stars visible on a clear night. This session calls our attention to the grandeur of creation as a way of reflecting on God's goodness, but it also challenges us to consider ourselves as part of a wondrous design, something larger and more profound than anything that might be consuming our attention as we move through our day-to-day routines. Leaders might begin by asking participants, for example, if anything in this session shifted their perspective? Or did anything put their daily responsibilities, anxieties, or expectations in new perspective?

Is your image of God changing at all?
A number of participants may come to *The Rescue Project* with preconceived notions of God (angry, judgmental, restricting, unfair, uncaring, disengaged, aloof, and maybe even non-existent, to name only a few.) One way to begin this conversation is to ask participants what their image of God was before they walked through the door today? A next step might be to ask how this session seems to present God, just to make sure everybody is seeing and hearing the same message. Then leaders might ask about how the image of God is shifting (if at all) for participants. In other words, "What do you see here that's new for you?"

Reflect quietly on what's causing you anxiety right now. How does the God of the Biblical Story impact that?
With this question it is perhaps best for leaders to reassure participants that nobody will be asked to share out with the group what it is they are thinking about in terms of anxieties and concerns. Simply invite them to place those things in the context of the material of this session and reflect on how they are feeling as a result.

DEEPER QUESTIONS

1. How have your impressions of The Bible been shaped?

2. If Genesis chapters 1-2 are meant to be read as inspired poetry, then how are we to know with any certainty what truths they are intended to reveal?

3. What is your relationship with God?

_____

_____

_____

_____

_____

_____

_____

_____

_____

RESOURCES

Catechism of the Catholic Church 295-301:
"The Mystery of Creation"

295 We believe that God created the world according to his wisdom. It is not the product of any necessity whatever, nor of blind fate or chance. We believe that it proceeds from God's free will; he wanted to make his creatures share in his being, wisdom and goodness: "For you created all things, and by your will they existed and were created." Therefore, the Psalmist exclaims: "O LORD, how manifold are your works! In wisdom you have made them all"; and "The LORD is good to all, and his compassion is over all that he has made."

God creates "out of nothing"

296 We believe that God needs no pre-existent thing or any help in order to create, nor is creation any sort of necessary emanation from the divine substance. God creates freely "out of nothing":

If God had drawn the world from pre-existent matter, what would be so extraordinary in that?

A human artisan makes from a given material whatever he wants, while God shows his power by starting from nothing to make all he wants.

297 Scripture bears witness to faith in creation "out of nothing" as a truth full of promise and hope. Thus, the mother of seven sons encourages them for martyrdom:

I do not know how you came into being in my womb. It was not I who gave you life and breath, nor I who set in order the elements within each of you. Therefore, the Creator of the world, who shaped the beginning of man and devised the origin of all things, will in his mercy give life and breath back to you again, since you now forget yourselves for the sake of his laws... Look at the heaven and the earth and see everything that is in them, and recognize that God did not make them out of things that existed. Thus, also mankind comes into being.

298 Since God could create everything out of nothing, he can also, through the Holy Spirit, give spiritual life to sinners by creating a pure heart in them, and bodily life to the dead through the Resurrection. God "gives life to the dead and calls into existence the things that do not exist" and since God was able to make light shine in darkness by his Word, he can also give the light of faith to those who do not yet know him.

God creates an ordered and good world

299 Because God creates through wisdom, his creation is ordered: "You have arranged all things by measure and number and weight." The universe, created in and by the eternal Word, the "image of the invisible God," is destined for and addressed to man, himself created in the "image of God" and called to a personal relationship

with God. Our human understanding, which shares in the light of the divine intellect, can understand what God tells us by means of his creation, though not without great effort and only in a spirit of humility and respect before the Creator and his work. Because creation comes forth from God's goodness, it shares in that goodness– "and God saw that it was good... very good"– for God willed creation as a gift addressed to man, an inheritance destined for and entrusted to him. On many occasions the Church has had to defend the goodness of creation, including that of the physical world.

God transcends creation and is present to it

300 God is infinitely greater than all his works: "You have set your glory above the heavens." Indeed, God's "greatness is unsearchable." But because he is the free and sovereign Creator, the first cause of all that exists, God is present to his creatures' inmost being: "In him we live and move and have our being." In the words of St. Augustine, God is "higher than my highest and more inward than my innermost self."

God upholds and sustains creation

301 With creation, God does not abandon his creatures to themselves. He not only gives them being and existence, but also, and at every moment, upholds and sustains them in being, enables them to act and brings them to their final end. Recognizing this utter dependence with respect to the Creator is a source of wisdom and freedom, of joy and confidence:

For you love all things that exist, and detest none of the things that you have made; for you would not have made anything if you had hated it. How would anything have endured, if you had not willed it? Or how would anything not called forth by you have been preserved? You spare all things, for they are yours, O Lord, you who love the living.[4]

SUGGESTED READING

Johnston, George. "How to Read the First Chapters of Genesis." *Lay Witness,* 1998.

Kreeft, Peter. *You Can Understand the Bible,* 2005.

Documents of Vatican II. "Dogmatic Constitution on Divine Revelation." *Dei Verbum,* 1965.

Pope Benedict XVI. *"In the Beginning...": A Catholic Understanding of the Story of Creation and the Fall,* 2013.

2. Ratzinger, *Credo for Today: What Christians Believe,* 37.

3. Gen. 1:16 RSV.

4. *Catechism of the Catholic Church,* 295-301: "The Mystery of Creation".

Chapter Three

The Enemy Is the Enemy

"The sight of these happy creatures filled the devil and his fallen angels with anger and envy. They took thought as to how they might mar the work of God and destroy the destiny of this newly created race. They set about to enslave those whom they had been meant to serve and to degrade those who had been assigned such an exalted place into the lowly slime beneath their feet." [5]

- Sophia Consulting,
The Christian Cosmic Narrative

THE GRACE: *Light*

But by the envy of the devil, Death entered the world, and those who are in his possession experience it.[6]

Wisdom 2:24

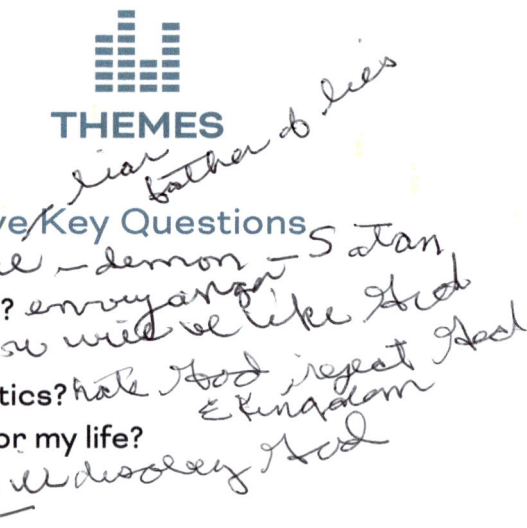

THEMES

The Enemy: Five Key Questions
- Who is he? ~~devil~~ — demon — Satan *liar, father of lies*
- Why did he rebel? envy, anger *you will be like God*
- What's his lie? you will be like God
- What are his tactics? hate God, reject God, E kingdom
- What's his goal for my life? *To do God's holy & true will,* disobey God

QUESTIONS TO CONSIDER

- Where is the enemy accusing me right now?
- What lie is crippling me right now?
- Where is the enemy causing division in my life right now?
- Where is the enemy flattering my ego right now?
- What temptation is strongest in my life right now?
- Where am I most discouraged right now?

_____

_____

_____

_____

_____

_____

_____

_____

_____

Facilitator Resources

Chapter Summary

The Catholic Church teaches that the human race has an enemy who is real, powerful beyond our imaginations, and singularly focused on our destruction. While we cannot defeat this enemy on our own, God has equipped us for spiritual warfare through Scripture with knowledge of his identity, his motives, and his tactics.

GOALS

- Grasp the fact that the "bad news" is truly horrific.

- Shine a light on the enemy, Satan, in order to understand precisely who he is and why he hates the human race.

- Expose his strategies of deception and his ultimate objective for you and me.

Chapter Topics

- Why the Universe Is Messed Up

- Scripture as Game Film

- The Enemy's Identity

- Recognizing the Enemy at Work in Our Lives

ACTION ITEMS

- Be sure to continue to include the pre-session and post-session *Rescue* huddles into your routine.

- Prepare participants for the fact that Session 4 will be just as difficult as Session 3 (maybe more so). But remind them that this material, as hard as it seems, is necessary in order to make absolutely clear why the good news of God's plan of salvation for the human race is so extraordinary.

- Continue to offer to make yourself available for coffee or a phone call or a conversation by email with participants who might have additional questions or feel the need to follow up with any of the content.

PASTORAL NOTES

1. The difficult content of Chapter Three Chapter Three (and Chapter Four, for that matter) is going to be hard, most especially perhaps in the way that participants are likely to respond to the crushing reality that we have a dangerous enemy who wants to destroy us. But this information is necessary for at least two reasons. First, the "bad news" helps us to understand why the "good news" of the gospel is so extraordinary. Second, if knowledge is power, then knowing who this enemy is and what he intends for us enables us to better contend with him. Encourage participants to hang in there because there is hope. Experience these next two sessions remembering that there is only one God and that he is good and without rival. The Lord is the One exposing this enemy of ours for our great benefit.

2. The reality of the enemy
Many people living in our modern world simply reject the notion that the devil exists, let alone that he could play havoc with our lives. Some in the Church even proclaim that the enemy is merely a symbol. But Jesus himself throughout the Gospels speaks often about the reality of the devil and the ways we must face him in the world. So be prepared to encounter participant skepticism about this aspect of the spiritual realm. A great place to start is with what the Catholic Church teaches about the devil by directing participants to paragraphs 391-395 of the Catechism of the Catholic Church provided

in the Resource section at the end of this chapter.

3. Recognizing participants' trauma

Because of the very personal nature of the content in Chapter Three (and Chapter Four), be prepared to encounter participants who have experienced trauma themselves and may respond in particular ways (appropriately so!) to these next two sessions. Abuse and human trafficking are far more common in our world today than any of us would like to think. Most dioceses have resources to offer, so reach out to the staff if you find yourself in a situation you do not feel comfortable handling alone.

QUESTIONS TO CONSIDER

Rather than guide a discussion here, leaders should encourage participants not only to reflect personally on each of these questions but also to write out their responses in the space provided in their guides. Again, reassure participants that they will not be required to share anything aloud.

Where is the enemy accusing me right now?

What lie is crippling me right now?

Where is the enemy causing division in my life right now?

Where is the enemy flattering my ego right now?

What temptation is strongest in my life right now?

Where am I most discouraged right now?

DEEPER QUESTIONS

1. Do you believe that the enemy is real?

2. In what ways has the enemy succeeded in convincing you of the lie that God is not a good Father?

3. Do you see your struggles with sin any differently after this chapter?

_____

_____

_____

_____

_____

_____

_____

RESOURCES

Catechism of the Catholic Church 391-395:
"The Fall of the Angels"

391 Behind the disobedient choice of our first parents lurks a seductive voice, opposed to God, which makes them fall into death out of envy. Scripture and the Church's Tradition see in this being a fallen angel, called "Satan" or the "devil." The Church teaches that Satan was at first a good angel, made by God: "The devil and the other demons were indeed created naturally good by God, but they became evil by their own doing."

392 Scripture speaks of a sin of these angels. This "fall" consists in the free choice of these created spirits, who radically and irrevocably rejected God and his reign. We find a reflection of that rebellion in the tempter's words to our first parents: "You will be like God." The devil "has sinned from the beginning"; he is "a liar and the father of lies."

393 It is the *irrevocable* character of their choice, and not a defect in the infinite divine mercy, that makes the angels' sin unforgivable. "There is no repentance for the angels after their fall, just as there is no repentance for men after death."

394 Scripture witnesses to the disastrous influence of

the one Jesus calls "a murderer from the beginning," who would even try to divert Jesus from the mission received from his Father. "The reason the Son of God appeared was to destroy the works of the devil." In its consequences the gravest of these works was the mendacious seduction that led man to disobey God.

395 The power of Satan is, nonetheless, not infinite. He is only a creature, powerful from the fact that he is pure spirit, but still a creature. He cannot prevent the building up of God's reign. Although Satan may act in the world out of hatred for God and his kingdom in Christ Jesus, and although his action may cause grave injuries—of a spiritual nature and, indirectly, even of a physical nature—to each man and to society, the action is permitted by divine providence which with strength and gentleness guides human and cosmic history. It is a great mystery that providence should permit diabolical activity, but "we know that in everything God works for good with those who love him." [7]

SUGGESTED READING

Lewis, C. S. *The Screwtape Letters,* 1942.

Spitzer, Fr. Robert. *Christ and Satan in Our Daily Lives,* 2020.

---

5. Sophia Consulting, *The Christian Cosmic Narrative,* 23.

6. *Lectionary for Mass,* 2002, Wisdom 2:24.

7. *Catechism of the Catholic Church* 391-395: "The Fall of the Angels."

Chapter Four

It Gets Worse

"The controlling metaphor of this section is slavery and freedom. Paul paints a black-or-white picture of the human situation: either one lives in service to sin and remains in spiritual bondage, or one lives in obedience to God and enjoys liberation from sin's captivity. It is a stark either-or: no fence-sitting, no third option." [8]

- Dr. Scott Hahn,
Commentary on Romans

THE GRACE: *Despair*

When a strongman, fully armed, guards his own palace, his goods are safe; but when one stronger than he attacks him and overcomes him, he takes away his armor in which he trusted and divides his spoil.

Luke 11:21-22

THEMES

The Strongman Parable

- The strongman – *the enemy*
- His palace – *the world*
- His goods – *humankind*
- The stronger one – *Jesus*

QUESTIONS TO CONSIDER

- What am I thinking and feeling right now?
- Did God reveal something new to me about how the enemy works in my life?
- How does the Biblical Story's vision that the enemy is the enemy (and that he divides and accuses) change the way I think about what is happening around me right now?

_____

_____

_____

_____

_____

_____

_____

_____

_____

_____

Facilitator Resources

Created | Captured | Rescued | Response

Chapter Summary

We are often taught that the result of the Fall as depicted in Genesis 3 is something that might solely be described as "separation from God." Chapter Four attempts to correct this fairly common misunderstanding and lays out in stark fashion the true horror of our reality. Sacred Scripture and Church tradition make clear that the human race, as a consequence of our rebellion, has sold itself into slavery to powers against which we cannot compete.

GOALS

● Really get why the "bad news" is horrifying.

● Appreciate the Biblical views of Sin, Death, and the enemy.

Chapter Topics

- The Consequences of the Fall

- The Captivity of Sin and Death

- The Enemy as Ruler of This World

ACTION ITEMS

- Use constructive comments from within your group discussion to move the conversation in fruitful directions.

- Worship is an essential element of The Rescue Project experience. Worship music may be live or played on a device by accessing Spotify, Amazon Music, or iTunes. Beautiful music helps facilitate an encounter with God.

- If participants are able and willing, consider meeting as a group outside of your regular weekly experience for a meal at a restaurant or someone's home. These gatherings can—but don't necessarily need to—extend your Rescue Project conversations.

PASTORAL NOTES

1. The difficult content continues with Chapter Four
Chapter Four continues to be hard, most especially perhaps in the way that participants are likely to respond to the crushing reality that we have a dangerous enemy who wants to destroy us. But this information, again, is necessary for at least two reasons. First, the "bad news" helps us to understand why the "good news" of the gospel is so extraordinary. Second, knowing who the enemy is and what he intends for us enables us to better contend with him. Encourage participants to hang in there because there is hope. Experience these next two sessions remembering that there is only one God and that he is good and without rival. The Lord is the One exposing this enemy of ours for our great benefit.

2. Content warning: Abuse and Trafficking
Be prepared to encounter participants who have experienced the trauma of abuse and human trafficking themselves and may respond in particular ways (appropriately so!) to these last two sessions. Tragically, abuse and human trafficking are much too common in the world today. Most dioceses have resources to offer, so reach out to the office staff if you find yourself in a situation you do not feel comfortable handling alone.

3. Hope is coming!

Once participants have been immersed in the "bad news" of Captured in Sessions 3 and 4, be sure to share that hope is coming. Let folks know that Chapters 5 and 6 launch the content of what we call Rescued— and that there is good reason to believe they might be overwhelmed (in the best sense of that description!) by the extraordinary news of the gospel.

QUESTIONS TO CONSIDER

What are you thinking and feeling right now?
This particular question is designed intentionally as an open-ended reflection. We encourage you to affirm what participants share and, if possible, to put their observations into conversation with each other. These types of discussions can at times be a little unwieldy, but they are also oftentimes the most rewarding for both individuals and the group.

Did God reveal something new to you about how the enemy works in your life?
It can be a liberating experience for participants to consider that many of the things they struggle with—anger, self-doubt, anxiety, an inability to leave the past behind—might be the work of that third actor on the stage. Remember, we want to shine a bright light on the enemy, revealing his identity and how he works with each of us as individuals.

How does the vision of the Biblical Story that the enemy is the enemy (and that he divides and accuses) change the way you think about what is happening around you right now?

As prideful as Satan is, one of his most effective tactics against us, we are taught, is getting us to focus on people and things other than himself. It lowers our guard, even to the point of forgetting (or disbelieving) that he is personally at war with us. So when we define citizens of another nation or members of a different political party or difficult colleagues at work or practitioners of another religious faith as "our enemy," we not only fall victim to his strategy of setting us against each other, we also leave ourselves even more vulnerable to his destructive designs.

DEEPER QUESTIONS

1. Have you ever struggled with the fact that God allows the enemy to reign over this world?

2. How do the Biblical teachings on Sin and Death as dominions alter your understanding of their roles in our lives?

3. Human powerlessness has been a theme the last few sessions. Does this shift, in any way, how you regard your faith?

_____

_____

_____

_____

_____

_____

_____

_____

RESOURCES

Freedom put to the test

396 God created man in his image and established him in his friendship. A spiritual creature, man can live this friendship only in free submission to God. The prohibition against eating "of the tree of the knowledge of good and evil" spells this out: "for in the day that you eat of it, you shall die." The "tree of the knowledge of good and evil" symbolically evokes the insurmountable limits that man, being a creature, must freely recognize and respect with trust. Man is dependent on his Creator, and subject to the laws of creation and to the moral norms that govern the use of freedom.

Man's first sin

397 Man, tempted by the devil, let his trust in his Creator die in his heart and, abusing his freedom, disobeyed God's command. This is what man's first sin consisted of. All subsequent sin would be disobedience toward God and lack of trust in his goodness.

398 In that sin man *preferred* himself to God and by that very act scorned him. He chose himself over and

against God, against the requirements of his creaturely status and therefore against his own good. Created in a state of holiness, man was destined to be fully "divinized" by God in glory. Seduced by the devil, he wanted to "be like God," but "without God, before God, and not in accordance with God."

399 Scripture portrays the tragic consequences of this first disobedience. Adam and Eve immediately lose the grace of original holiness. They become afraid of the God of whom they have conceived a distorted image–that of a God jealous of his prerogatives.

400 The harmony in which they had found themselves, thanks to original justice, is now destroyed: the control of the soul's spiritual faculties over the body is shattered; the union of man and woman becomes subject to tensions, their relations henceforth marked by lust and domination. Harmony with creation is broken: visible creation has become alien and hostile to man. Because of man, creation is now subject "to its bondage to decay." Finally, the consequence explicitly foretold for this disobedience will come true: man will "return to the ground," for out of it he was taken.

Death makes its entrance into human history

401 After that first sin, the world is virtually inundated by sin. There is Cain's murder of his brother Abel and the universal corruption which follows in the wake of sin. Likewise, sin frequently manifests itself in the history of Israel, especially as infidelity to the God of the

Covenant and as transgression of the Law of Moses. And even after Christ's atonement, sin raises its head in countless ways among Christians. Scripture and the Church's Tradition continually recall the presence and *universality of sin in man's history*:

What Revelation makes known to us is confirmed by our own experience. For when man looks into his own heart he finds that he is drawn towards what is wrong and sunk in many evils which cannot come from his good creator. Often refusing to acknowledge God as his source, man has also upset the relationship which should link him to his last end, and at the same time he has broken the right order that should reign within himself as well as between himself and other men and all creatures. [9]

SUGGESTED READING

Rutledge, Fleming. *The Crucifixion: Understanding the Death of Jesus,* 2015.

---

8. Hahn, *Commentary on Romans,* 102.
9. *Catechism of the Catholic Church* 396-401: "Original Sin."

Chapter Five

Why Did Jesus Come?

"Lord God Almighty, who sent Your Only Begotten Son to endow humankind, imprisoned in slavery to Sin, with the freedom of Your sons and daughters, we pray most humbly for these children, whom You know will experience the allurements of this world, and will fight against the snares of the devil: by the power of the Passion and Resurrection of Your Son deliver them now from the stain of Original Sin, strengthen them with the grace of Christ, and guard them always on their journey through life." [10]

- Baptismal Ritual of the Catholic Church

THE GRACE: *Light*

For thus says the Lord:
"Even the captives of the mighty shall be taken, and the prey of the tyrant be rescued, for I will contend with those who contend with you, and I will save your children. . . .Then all flesh shall know that I am the Lord your Savior, and your Redeemer, the Mighty One of Jacob."

Isaiah 49:25-26

THEMES

What was Jesus *doing* on the cross?
1. Showing us the love of the Father.
2. Making atonement; becoming Sin.
3. Going to war to rescue us.

QUESTIONS TO CONSIDER

- What am I thinking and how am I feeling now?
- How does the story of Jesus as a warrior coming to rescue me change how I see him?
- Does understanding that Jesus didn't only do this for me change how I see and treat others?

_____

_____

_____

_____

_____

_____

_____

_____

_____

_____

Facilitator Resources

Created | Captured | *Rescued* | Response

Chapter Summary

Chapter Five continues our examination of the Biblical Story with the question, "What was the life and death of Jesus all about?" Did He come merely to tell stories, exhort us to be kind and love one another, perform a few miracles, and then meet a tragic premature end? He did all these things, to be sure, but these aren't the reasons He came. Jesus became man to rescue the creature He loves most—not just humanity, generally, but you and me, personally. And He did all of that in a most extraordinarily creative and fitting way, for the one who deceived our race at its beginning was himself deceived into bringing about the ruin of his own kingdom.

GOALS

- Recognize why Jesus came.
- Understand what Jesus was doing on the cross.

Chapter Topics

- The Incarnation as Invasion

- Jesus as Warrior

- The Personal Nature of Jesus's Victory

ACTION ITEMS

- By this point in *The Rescue Project* experience, your group will probably have formed its own unique rhythms during sessions discussions. As long as certain individuals are not dominating conversations and/or others are being left out, step back a little and try to allowthe dialogue between participants to develop more organically.

- As you continue to open and close each session with prayer, consider asking participants if they would like to step in and lead prayer for the group. Don't be discouraged if folks are reluctant at first. Respect their apprehension and continue to offer at later sessions.

PASTORAL NOTES

1. The kind, gentle, and inclusive Jesus

Many participants will bring with them to *The Rescue Project* experience an understandably limited notion of Jesus as simply kind, gentle, and inclusive. This, after all, is what many of us were taught in religious education classes and have subsequently encountered in popular culture. While Jesus is certainly all of these things (blessed be HE!), Scripture makes clear that He is so much more. As much as anything, the New Testament presents Jesus as powerful, authoritative, and demanding: He walked on water, fed five thousand people with a few loaves of bread, and brought the dead back to life; He drove out demons, commanded them to be silent, and vanquished Satan; He welcomed sinners, exhorted them to repentance, but did not soften his teaching when individuals found the expectations to be too much. In short, when contemporaries of Jesus met Him, they generally had one of two radical responses: they either dropped everything to follow Him or they wanted to kill Him. No one ever yawned, shrugged, or found him just to be a nice person. The constant response of the crowds was shock and awe.

2. Jesus the ambush predator?

The idea that Jesus on the cross is the aggressor and the hunter will sound strange to many. But direct participants to the Resources section at the end of this chapter, where they will see for themselves that this was a frequent way that the early Church preached about Jesus's work on the cross. Everyone from St. Melito of Sardis to St. Irenaeus to St. Gregory of Nyssa to St. Ephrem to St. Augustine (to name only a few) presents Jesus as a warrior, fighting for us (in many cases by baiting the enemy), and binding the "strong man."

QUESTIONS TO CONSIDER

What are you thinking and how are you feeling now?
As in the previous session's discussion, this particular question is designed intentionally as an open-ended reflection. We encourage you to affirm what participants share and, if possible, to put their observations into conversation with each other. These types of discussions can at times be a little unwieldy but they are also oftentimes the most rewarding for both individuals and the group.

How does the Story of Jesus as a warrior coming to rescue you change how you see Him?
Many participants will likely begin by remarking, "I've never been taught any of this!" Try to encourage the discussion by asking initial follow-up questions like, "what's the most interesting part of all of this for you?" or "what seems most strange?" Once everyone has expressed their surprise with the content, leaders can guide the group to those teachings and Scripture

passages that corroborate, seemingly indisputably, the notion of Jesus coming to fight for each of us. Ideally, getting participants to reflect on their ultimate conception of Jesus—and how that might transform their understanding of salvation, itself—is the goal here.

Understanding that Jesus didn't only do this for you, does that change how you see and treat others?
This question is designed in part to prompt participants to begin integrating the individual parts of the story into something larger and applying it to the way they live their lives. Personal transformation and mobilization is what *The Rescue Project* is all about. Ask participants to think in terms of before/after ("Before I might have thought of things this way, but now...") and invite them to imagine hypothetical situations where they might enact the transformation they're experiencing.

DEEPER QUESTIONS

1. What aspect of Jesus' humanity is most difficult for you to reconcile with his divinity?

2. How was your understanding of the meaning of the crucifixion formed?

3. Who among the early Church Fathers included in the Resource section of this chapter presents the most powerful argument for Jesus as warrior?

_____

_____

_____

_____

_____

_____

_____

_____

_____

RESOURCES

The Greatest Philosopher Who Ever Lived, Peter Kreeft.

"The first question a child asks about a story is: What is it about? Is it a love story, a war story, an adventure story, a psychological drama, or what? The question presupposes that there is an answer to it and that the author of the story knows the answer, that he is in charge, that he knows what kind of story he is telling...

"In one sense, the story of human history is a love story. But in a fallen world, a love story is always also a war story. In fact, the single fundamental theme of every story since the Fall has always been the war between good and evil. That is the theme of the Bible, especially in the last book, Revelation, which symbolically summarizes and interprets all the little stories in terms of the big story...

"God Himself announces this theme, within the story itself. For this God, unlike the God of deism, reveals Himself to us. In fact, he makes himself a character in the story as well as being the transcendent Author of it...

"Immediately after the Fall, which is the beginning of human history, he announces the theme of his story, of history. It is war: 'I will put enmity [war] between you [Satan] and the Woman [Eve]...'

"This is the first Gospel, the 'proto-evangelium.' Strange as it sounds, the Gospel is a war story. No one can read the four Gospels alertly and intelligently and open-mindedly without seeing that. The 'liberal' point that Jesus was simply to teach love is about as accurate as the idea that the purpose of Adolf Hitler was to create world peace. For in a fallen world, the only way that there can be love is for there to be war. Love wars. Love fights. Ask any mother, in any species of mammal, especially homo sapiens.

"Christ versus Antichrist, the City of God versus the City of This World, the Holy Spirit and His angels versus the Devil and his fallen angels, light versus darkness, good versus evil - that is the plot...

"The warfare, of course, is spiritual in its root and in its essence. 'We are not contending against flesh and blood, but against the principalities, against the powers, against the world rulers of this present darkness' (Eph. 6:12)." [11]

Selected Writings of the Early Church Fathers on the Paschal Mystery

St. Ignatius of Antioch *(c. 50-110)*
There was concealed from the ruler of this world the virginity of Mary and the birth of our Lord, and the three renowned mysteries which were done in the tranquility of God from the star. And here, at the manifestation of the Son, magic began to be destroyed, and all bonds

were loosed; and the ancient kingdom and the error of evil was destroyed. Henceforward all things were moved together, and the destruction of death was devised, and there was the commencement of that which was perfected in God. [12]

St. Justin Martyr (c. 100-165)

Christ became man by the Virgin, in order that the disobedience that proceeded from the serpent might receive its destruction in the same manner in which it derived its origin. For Eve, who was a virgin and undefiled, having conceived the word of the serpent, brought forth disobedience and death. But the Virgin Mary received faith and joy when the angel Gabriel announced the good tidings to her that the Spirit of the Lord would come upon her, and the power of the Highest would overshadow her: wherefore also the Holy Thing begotten of her is the Son of God; and she replied, "Be it unto me according to Thy word" (Lk 1:38). And by her has He been born, to Whom we have proved so many Scriptures refer, and by Whom God destroys both the serpent and those angels and men who are like him. [13]

St. Melito of Sardis (c. 120-185)

Who is he who contends with Me? Let him stand in opposition to Me. I set the condemned man free; I gave the dead man life; I raised up the one who had been entombed. Who is My opponent? I, He says, am the Christ. I am the One who destroyed death, and triumphed over the enemy, and trampled Hades under foot, and bound the strong one, and carried off man to the heights of heaven. I, he says, am the Christ. This is the alpha and the omega. This is the beginning and the end—an indescribable beginning and an incomprehensible end. This is the Christ. This is the King. This is Jesus. This is the General. This is the Lord. This is the One who rose up from the dead. This is the One who sits at the right hand of the Father. [14]

———————

St. Irenaeus (c. 130-202)

Let us, then, put the question again: For what purpose did Christ come down from heaven?

Answer: "That He might destroy sin, overcome death, and give life to man." By the side of this pregnant saying we will set another, chosen from among many similar passages, which develops the dramatic idea in fuller detail: "Man had been created by God that he might have life. If now, having lost life, and having been harmed by the serpent, he were not to return to life, but were to be wholly abandoned to death, then God would have been defeated, and the malice of the serpent would have overcome God's will. But since God is both invincible and magnanimous, he showed his magnanimity in correcting man, and in proving all men, as we have said; but through the Second Man he bound the strong one, and spoiled his goods, and annihilated death, bringing life to man who had become subject to death. For Adam had become the devil's possession, and the devil held him under his power, by having wrongfully practiced deceit upon him, and by the offer of immortality made him subject to death. For by promising that they should be as gods, which did not lie in his power, he worked death in them. Wherefore he who had taken man captive was himself taken captive by God, and man who had been taken captive was set free from the bondage of condemnation."

"The Word of God," he says, "was made flesh in order that He might destroy death and bring man to life; for we were tied and bound in sin, we were born in sin and live under the dominion of death." [15]

St. Gregory of Nyssa (c. 335-395)

He was about to engage him who had taken human nature prisoner and was about to loosen death's bonds; by having destroyed the last enemy [cf. 1 Cor. 15:26], he might restore mankind to freedom and peace.

In order to secure that the ransom in our behalf might be easily accepted by him who required it, the Deity was hidden under the veil of our nature, that so, as with ravenous fish, the hook of the Deity might be gulped down along with the bait of flesh, and thus, life being introduced into the house of death, and light shining in darkness, that which is diametrically opposed to light and life might vanish; for it is not in the nature of darkness to remain when light is present, or of death to exist when life is active. [16]

St. Augustine (c.354-430)

The devil jumped for joy when Christ died; and by the very death of Christ the devil was overcome: he took, as it were, the bait in the mousetrap. He rejoiced at the death, thinking himself death's commander. But that which caused his joy dangled the bait before him. The Lord's cross was the devil's mousetrap: the bait which caught him was the death of the Lord.

The next verse explains something of the reason why so much honor should be paid to him, and why all nations should serve him: He has delivered the needy from the tyrant, that poor person who had no other champion. This needy and poor person is the people that believes in him, and within this people are kings who worship him. They are not too proud to be needy and poor, which means humbly acknowledging that they are sinners and in need of the glory of God, so that the true King, the Son of the King, may free them from the powerful foe. Powerful indeed he is who has been called the accuser. Yet it was not his own strength that brought men and women into subjection to this powerful tyrant, and kept them there in captivity, but human sins. The powerful tyrant is also called in scripture "the strong man," but Christ, who humiliated the accuser, also broke into the strong man's domain to bind him and seize his possessions. Christ is the one who has delivered the needy from the tyrant, that poor person who had no other champion, for no one else had the strength to accomplish that– no righteous person nor even any angel. There was no champion at all, therefore; but Christ came and saved them.

Having despoiled the devil, Christ distributes his gifts to beautify the Church. The psalm proceeds: It is the Beloved's part also to divide the spoils for the beauty of the house. The word Beloved is repeated for emphasis. But in fact it is not all the codices that have this repetition, and the more exact among them prefix a star to it. Such signs are called asterisks, and they inform us that the passages so marked are present in the Hebrew, but not in the interpretation by the Septuagint. But whether we think Beloved was repeated, or was written once only, I think we must take the words that follow it, to divide the spoils for the beauty of the house, in the sense, it is the Beloved's part also to divide the spoils for the beauty of the house; that is, he was chosen also for the division of the spoils. Undoubtedly the Church which Christ has created is a beautiful house, and he has adorned it by distributing his spoils to it, as a body is made beautiful by the due distribution of its limbs. Now the word "spoils" is used of goods seized from vanquished enemies, and the gospel throws light on this passage by saying, No one can get into a strong man's house and carry off his implements, unless he has tied up the strong man first (Mt. 12:29). Christ tied up the devil with spiritual chains by overcoming death and ascending from the underworld to heaven; he bound the devil by the sacrament of his incarnation, because although the devil found nothing in Christ that deserved death, he was nonetheless allowed to kill him. The consequence was that Christ tied up the devil and took away his belongings as booty. These were the unbelievers through whom the devil worked his will. But the Lord cleansed these tools by forgiving their sins; he left the enemy felled and chained, and sanctified the spoils he had seized. He then assigned them to their due places for the adornment of his own house, appointing some to be apostles, some prophets, some pastors and teachers for the work of ministry, for the building up of the body of Christ.

We are thy servants, we are thy creatures: Thou hast made us, thou hast redeemed us. Anyone can buy his servant, create him he cannot; but the Lord hath both created and redeemed his servants; created them, that they might be; redeemed them, that they might not be captives ever. For we fell into the hands of the prince of this world, who seduced Adam, and made him his servant, and began to possess us as his slaves. But the Redeemer came, and the seducer was overcome. And what did our Redeemer to him who held us captive? For our ransom he held out his cross as a trap; he placed in It as a bait his blood. He indeed had power to shed his blood, he did not attain to drink it. And in that he shed the blood of him who was no debtor, he was commanded to render up the debtors; he shed the blood of the Innocent, he was commanded to withdraw from the guilty. He verily shed his blood to this end, that he might wipe out our sins. That then whereby he held us fast was effaced by the Redeemer's blood. For he only held us fast by the bonds of our own sins. They were the captive's chains. He came, he bound the strong one with the bonds of his passion; He entered into his house, into the hearts, that is, of those where he did dwell, and took away his vessels. We are his vessels. He had filled then with his own bitterness. This bitterness too he pledged to our Redeemer in the gall. He had filled us then as his vessels; but our Lord spoiling his vessels, and making them his own, poured out the bitterness, filled them with sweetness. [17]

St. Ephrem (c. 306-373)

Death trampled our Lord underfoot, but he in his turn treated death as a highroad for his own feet. He submitted to it, enduring it willingly, because by this means he would be able to destroy death in spite of itself.

Death had its own way when our Lord went out from Jerusalem carrying his cross; but when by a loud cry from that cross he summoned the dead from the underworld, death was powerless to prevent it.

Death slew him by means of the body which he had assumed, but that same body proved to be the weapon with which he conquered death. Concealed beneath the cloak of his manhood, his godhead engaged death in combat; but in slaying our Lord, death itself was slain. It was able to kill natural human life, but was itself killed by the life that is above the nature of man.

Death could not devour our Lord unless he possessed a body, neither could hell swallow him up unless he bore our flesh; and so he came in search of a chariot in which to ride to the underworld. This chariot was the body which he received from the Virgin; in it he invaded death's fortress, broke open its strong-room and scattered all its treasure. [18]

St. John Chrysostom (c. 347-407)

Whosoever is pious and loves God, let him enjoy this good and cheerful festival. Whosoever is a grateful servant, let him rejoice and enter into the joy of the Lord. Whosoever is weary of fasting, let him now receive his earnings. Whosoever has laboured from the first hour, let him today accept his just reward. Whosoever has come after the third hour, let him with thanksgiving take part in the celebration. Whosoever has arrived after the sixth hour, let him have no misgivings, for he too shall suffer no loss. Whosoever has delayed until the ninth hour, let him approach without hesitation. Whosoever has arrived only at the eleventh hour, let him not fear the delay, for the Master is gracious: He receives the last even as the first; He gives rest to him that comes at the eleventh hour, as well as to him that has laboured from the first; and to him that delayed he gives mercy, and the first he restores to health; to the one he gives, to the other he bestows.

And he accepts the works, and embraces the contemplation; the deed he honours, and the intention he commends.

Therefore let everyone enter into the joy of the Lord. The first and the last, receive your wages. Rich and poor, dance with each other. The temperate and the slothful, honour this day. Ye who have fasted and ye who have not, rejoice this day. The table is fully laden; all of you delight in it. The calf is plenteous, let no one depart hungry. Let everyone enjoy this banquet of faith. Let everyone take pleasure in the wealth of goodness. Let no one lament his poverty, for the universal kingdom has appeared. Let no one bewail for his transgressions, for forgiveness has risen from the grave. Let no one fear death, for the Saviours death has set us free. He who was held by death, eradicated death. He plundered Hades when He descended into Hades. He embittered it, when it tasted of his flesh, and this being foretold by Isaiah when he cried: Hades said it was embittered, when it encountered Thee below. Embittered, for it was abolished. Embittered, for it was ridiculed. Embittered, for it was put to death. Embittered, for it was dethroned. Embittered, for it was made captive.

It received a body and by chance came face to face with God. It received earth and encountered heaven. It received that which it could see, and was overthrown by him whom he could not see. Where, O death, is your sting? Where, O Hades, is your victory? Christ is risen, and thou art cast down. Christ is risen, and the demons have fallen. Christ is risen, and the angels rejoice. Christ is risen, and life is liberated. Christ is risen, and no one remains dead in a tomb. For Christ having risen from the dead, has become the first-fruits of those that have fallen asleep. To him be glory and power, for ever and ever.
Amen. [19]

St. Leo the Great (c. 400-461)
When, therefore, the merciful and almighty Saviour so arranged the commencement of His human course as to hide the power of his Godhead which was insepara-

ble from his manhood under the veil of our weakness, the crafty foe was taken off his guard and he thought that the nativity of the child, who was born for the salvation of mankind, was as much subject to himself as all others are at their birth. For he saw him crying and weeping, he saw him wrapped in swaddling clothes, subjected to circumcision, offering the sacrifice which the law required. And then he perceived in him the usual growth of boyhood, and could have had no doubt of His reaching man's estate by natural steps.

Meanwhile, he inflicted insults, multiplied injuries, made use of curses, affronts, blasphemies, abuse, in a word, poured upon him all the force of his fury and exhausted all the varieties of trial: and knowing how he had poisoned man's nature, had no conception that he had no share in the first transgression whose mortality he had ascertained by so many proofs. The unscrupulous thief and greedy robber persisted in assaulting Him Who had nothing of his own, and in carrying out the general sentence on original sin, went beyond the bond on which he rested, and required the punishment of iniquity from him in whom he found no fault. And thus the malevolent terms of the deadly compact are annulled, and through the injustice of an overcharge the whole debt is cancelled. The strong one is bound by his own chains, and every device of the evil one recoils on his own head. When the prince of the world is bound, all that he held in captivity is released. Our nature cleansed from its old contagion regains its honourable estate, death is destroyed by death, nativity is restored by nativity: since at one and the same time redemption does away with slavery, regeneration changes our origin, and faith justifies the sinner. [20]

The Council of Chalcedon (451)

His birth in time in no way subtracts from or adds to that divine and eternal birth of his: but its whole purpose is to restore humanity, who had been deceived, so that it might defeat death and, by its power, destroy the devil who held the power of death. Overcoming the originator of sin and death would be beyond us, had not he whom sin could not defile, nor could death hold down, taken up our nature and made it his own. He was conceived from the Holy Spirit inside the womb of the virgin mother. Her virginity was as untouched in giving him birth as it was in conceiving him. [21]

St. Isidore of Seville (c. 560-636)

The devil was deluded by the death of the Lord... for through the visible mortality of his flesh, Christ—whom the devil was trying to kill—concealed his divinity, like a snare in which he might entangle him like an unwise bird by a clever trick...The devil, although he attacked the flesh of the humanity in Christ that was evident, was captured as if by the fishhook of his divinity that was lying hidden. For there is in Christ the fishhook of divinity; the food, however, is the flesh; the fishing line is the genealogy that is recited by the Gospel. Holding this fishing line truly is God the Father. [22]

St. Maximus the Confessor (c. 580-662)

His flesh was set before that voracious, gaping dragon as bait to provoke him: flesh that would be deadly for the dragon, for it would utterly destroy him by the power of the Godhead hidden within it. For human nature, however, his flesh was to be a remedy since the power of the Godhead in it would restore human nature to its original grace.

Just as the devil had poisoned the tree of knowledge and spoiled our nature by its taste, so too, in presuming to devour the Lord's flesh he himself is corrupted and is completely destroyed by the power of the Godhead hidden in it. [23]

St. Bernard (c. 1090-1153)

He comes as an Infant, and without speech, for the voice of the wailing infant arouses compassion, not terror. If He is terrible to any, yet not to thee. He is become a Little One, his Virgin Mother swathes His tender limbs with bands, and dost thou still tremble with fear? By this weakness thou mayest know that He comes not to destroy, but to save; not to bind, but to unbind. If He shall take up the sword, it will be against thine enemies, and, as the Power and the Wisdom of God, He will trample on the necks of the proud and the mighty. We have two enemies, sin and death—that is, the death of the soul and the death of the body. Jesus comes to conquer both, and to save us from both. Already he has vanquished sin in his own person by assuming a human nature free from the corruption of sin. For great violence was offered to sin, and it knew itself to be indeed subdued, when that nature which it gloried to have wholly infected and possessed was found in Christ perfectly free from its dominion. Henceforth Christ will pursue our enemies, and will seize them, and will not desist until they are overcome in us. His whole mortal life was a war against sin. He fought against it by word and example. But it was in his passion that he came upon the strong man armed, and bound him, and bore away his spoils.

Jesus Christ also conquers our second enemy, death. He overcomes it first in himself, when he rises from the dead, the first-fruits of them that sleep, and the first-born from the dead. Afterwards he will, in like manner, vanquish death in all of us when He shall raise our mortal bodies from the dust, and destroy this our last enemy. Thus, when he rose from the dead, Jesus was clothed in beauty, not wrapped in swaddling-clothes as at his birth. He that previously overflowed with mercy, "judging no man," girded himself in His resurrection with the girdle of justice, and in so doing seemed in some degree to restrain His superabundant mercy in order to be thenceforth prepared for the judgment which is to follow our future resurrection. [24]

St. Bonaventure (c. 1221-1274)

Now that the combat of the passion was over, and the bloody dragon and raging lion thought that he had secured a victory by killing the Lamb, the power of the divinity began to shine forth in his soul as it descended into hell. By this power our strong Lion of the tribe of

Judah (Apoc. 5:5), rising against the strong man who was fully armed (Luke 11:21), tore the prey away from him, broke down the gates of hell and bound the serpent. Disarming the Principalities and Powers, he led them away boldly, displaying them openly in triumph in himself (Col. 2:15). Then the Leviathan was led about with a hook (Job 40:25), his jaw pierced by Christ so that he who had no right over the Head which he had attacked, also lost what he had seemed to have over the body. Then the true Samson, as he died, laid prostrate an army of the enemy (cf. Judges 16:30). Then the Lamb without stain by the blood of his Testament led forth the prisoners from the pit in which there was no water (Zach. 9:11).

Then the long-awaited brightness of a new light shone upon those that dwelt in the region of the shadow of death (Isa. 9:2). [25]

Did the devil know who Jesus was?

This often causes confusion, as it appears as though he does. Comments in the Gospels like, "We know who you are, the holy one of God," or "If you are the Son of God," seem to indicate that the devil and or the demons knew him. But this is not true. For one thing, love and humility are literally beyond hell's way of thinking, and God becoming flesh in the person of Jesus is the utmost in love and humility. Too, expressions like "holy one of God" or "Son of God" were common ways among the Jewish people of referring to the Messiah, who was not at all expected to be a divine person but rather a man.

Frank Sheed, in his book *To Know Christ Jesus,* puts it this way: "I think it was of the first urgency to find out what 'son of God' meant. It had been used in the Old Testament as a name for the Messiah (Ps. 2:7).

But did he know what it *meant?* 'Son of God' had been variously used in the Old Testament–of the chosen people, for instance (Ex. 4:22), and, in the plural, of the Jewish judges (Ps. 81:6). Satan knew his Old Testament, but the book of Job he must have scrutinized for special closeness, for so much of it was about a certain Satan and the high carnival he had at Job's expense. In that book (1:6, 2:1, 38:7) 'sons of God' meant the unfallen angels. Satan may well have weighed the possibility that the Messiah might be an angel, entering in some unforeseeable way into humanity for "the crushing of his head." [26]

10. *Baptismal Ritual of the Catholic Church*, 158.

11. Kreeft, *The Greatest Philosopher Who Ever Lived*, 247-248.

12. St. Ignatius of Antioch, "The Second Epistle of Ignatius to the Ephesians," 102.

13. St. Justin Martyr, "Dialogue with Trypho," 100.

14. St. Melito of Sardis, "Sermon on The Passover."

15. St. Irenaeus, *The Demonstration of the Apostolic Preaching.*

16. St. Gregory of Nyssa, *The Great Catechism,* ch. XXIV.

17. St. Augustine, "Expositions of the Psalms 51-72," 464-465.

18. St. Ephrem, "A Sermon on the Cross of Christ."

19. St. John Chrysostom, "The Easter Sermon of John Chrysostom."

20. St. Leo the Great, *"Sermon 22."*

21. The Council of Chalcedon. "The Letter of Pope Leo to Flavian."

22. Knoebel quoting Isidore of *Seville, Sententiae,* 61.

23. St. Maximus the Confessor, *Mystery of the Divine Incarnation.*

24. St. Bernard, "The Fountains of the Savior," *Sermons on Advent & Christmas,* 103-104.

25. St. Bonaventure, *The Soul's Journey to God,* 159.

26. Sheed, *To Know Christ Jesus,* 118.

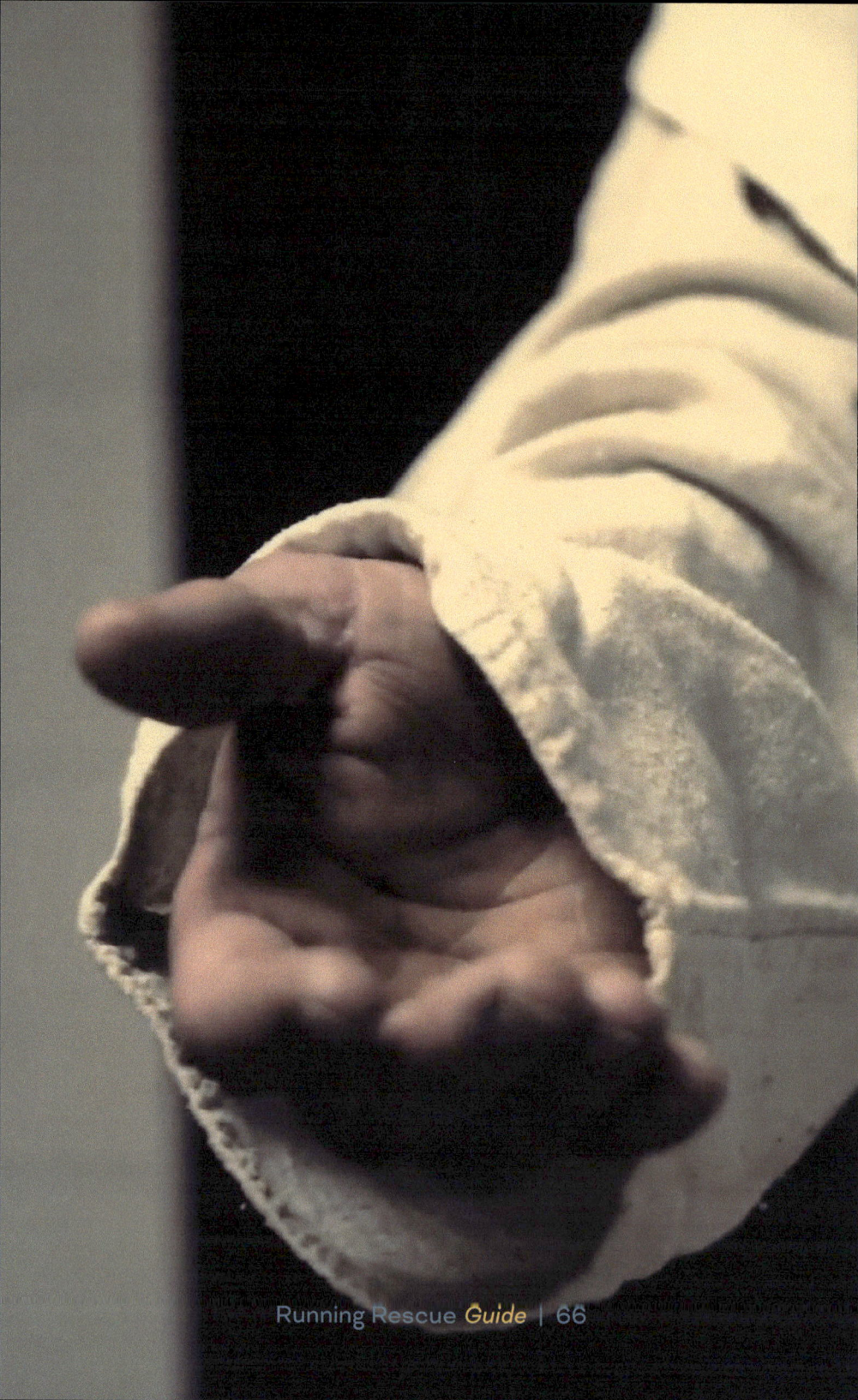

Chapter Six

What Difference Does It Make?

"Let no one fear death, for the Death of our Savior has set us free. He has destroyed it by enduring it. He destroyed Hades when He descended into it. He put it into an uproar even as it tasted of His flesh. Isaiah foretold this when he said, 'You, O Hell, have been troubled by encountering Him below.' Hell was in an uproar because it was done away with. It was in an uproar because it is mocked. It was in an uproar, for it is destroyed. It is in an uproar, for it is annihilated. It is in an uproar, for it is now made captive. Hell took a body, and discovered God. It took earth, and encountered Heaven. It took what it saw, and was over-come by what it did not see. O death, where is thy sting? O Hades, where is thy victory?" [27]

- St. John Chrysostom

THE GRACE:
Unshakeable Confidence in Jesus

For he rescued us from the domain of Darkness, and transferred us to the kingdom of his beloved Son, in whom we have redemption, the forgiveness of sins. [28]

Colossians 1:13-14

THEMES

Jesus has...

- Humiliated the enemy.
- Transferred humanity from one dominion to another.
- Rendered Sin impotent.
- Destroyed the power of Death.
- Canceled our debt.
- Recreated us.
- Given us access to the Father.
- Given us authority over the enemy.
- Sent us on mission to get his world back.
- Divinized us.

QUESTIONS TO CONSIDER

- What am I thinking and how am I feeling right now?
- Which result of the resurrection of Jesus resonates most deeply with me and why?
- Calling to mind the importance of stories from Chapter One, what impact is the biblical story having on my life?

_____

_____

_____

_____

_____

_____

_____

_____

_____

_____

Facilitator Resources

Chapter Summary

The Catholic Church teaches that Christ's victory on the cross finds its fulfillment in the resurrection. But what exactly does that mean? The short answer, of course, is that Jesus' dying and rising from the dead changed everything: we have been re-made as individuals and as a race and sent on mission by God to participate in the recreation of His world.

GOALS

- Understand the full significance of Jesus' resurrection.

- Appreciate the very personal nature of what that transformation means.

Chapter Topics

- Jesus Has Triumphed Over Our Enemies
- The Human Race Has Been Re-Created
- We Have a Mission

ACTION ITEMS

- By this point in *The Rescue Project* experience, your group will probably have formed its own unique rhythms during sessions discussions. As long as certain individuals are not dominating conversations and/or others are being left out, step back a little and try to allow the dialogue between participants to develop more organically.

- As you continue to open and close each session with prayer, consider asking participants if they would like to step in and lead prayer for the group. Don't be discouraged if folks are reluctant at first. Respect their apprehension and continue to offer at later sessions.

PASTORAL NOTES

1. What does "being sent on mission" mean?

Participants are going to begin hearing more and more about "being sent on mission" in the second half of *The Rescue Project*. Reassure them if the topic comes up that they are not being asked to do anything they might be uncomfortable with. Jesus commissioned all of us—not just the apostles, but all of us—to be heralds of the gospel. God desires everyone to know about His rescue because He desires everyone to be saved. The last three sessions will make clear for everyone what the opportunities are for being heralds of the gospel, the mission portion of our response to having been rescued.

2. Retreat is coming!

Prepare participants for the fact that the next two sessions (Chapters 7 and 8) comprise the retreat segment of *The Rescue Project*. The retreat is the capstone of the experience that allows an opportunity for participants to respond to all God has done for them. Provide the group with a general overview of the half-day experience, explaining the basics of what to expect at a retreat (prayer, worship, reflection) and how it might compare to what they've encountered in the regular Rescue sessions.

QUESTIONS TO CONSIDER

What are you thinking and how are you feeling right now?

Again, this particular question is designed intentionally as an open-ended reflection. We encourage you to affirm what participants share and, if possible, to put their observations into conversation with each other. These types of discussions can at times be a little unwieldy but they are also oftentimes the most rewarding for both individuals and the group.

Which result of the resurrection of Jesus resonates most deeply with you and why?

Participants will rely on an entire range of rationales for their choices here. As with any discussion, listen first, affirm second, and follow up with a question or two (if appropriate), always mindful of expanding the conversation to include others.

Calling to mind the importance of stories from Chapter One ("From grand cosmic myths to intimate family tales, it is in stories that we find meaning, purpose, and the truths by which we live…"), what impact is the Biblical Story having on your life?

Answers to this question will span from the very specific ("I understand the reason Jesus died on the cross a little better," or "I never considered that the devil was actually real") to the extremely general ("I'm starting to see how it all fits together," or "I feel differently than I did at the beginning of *The Rescue Project*"). One suggestion is to lead participants from specifics to generalities and from generalities to specifics with affirmations and follow ups. Don't be afraid to put different responses in conversation with each other by pointing out, for example, what one participant says and how that might relate to another's comment.

DEEPER QUESTIONS

1. Have you ever considered that Jesus' resurrection brought with it expectations for you personally?

2. What does "having access to the Father" mean to you?

3. Has *The Rescue Project* notion of being rescued by God transformed your understanding of being a Christian?

_____

_____

_____

_____

_____

RESOURCES

Catechism of the Catholic Church 651-655:
"The Meaning and Saving Significance of the Resurrection"

651 "If Christ has not been raised, then our preaching is in vain and your faith is in vain." The Resurrection above all constitutes the confirmation of all Christ's works and teachings. All truths, even those most inaccessible to human reason, find their justification if Christ by his Resurrection has given the definitive proof of his divine authority, which he had promised.

652 Christ's Resurrection is the fulfillment of the promises both of the Old Testament and of Jesus himself during his earthly life. The phrase "in accordance with the Scriptures" indicates that Christ's Resurrection fulfilled these predictions.

653 The truth of Jesus' divinity is confirmed by his Resurrection. He had said: "When you have lifted up the Son of man, then you will know that I am he." The Resurrection of the crucified one shows that he was truly "I AM," the Son of God and God himself.

So St. Paul could declare to the Jews: "What God promised to the fathers, this he has fulfilled to us their children by raising Jesus; as also it is written in the second psalm, 'You are my Son, today I have begotten you.'" Christ's Resurrection is closely linked to the Incarnation of God's Son, and is its fulfillment in accordance with God's eternal plan.

654 The Paschal mystery has two aspects: by his death, Christ liberates us from sin; by his Resurrection, he opens for us the way to a new life. This new life is above all justification that reinstates us in God's grace, "so that as Christ was raised from the dead by the glory of the Father, we too might walk in newness of life." Justification consists in both victory over the death caused by sin and a new participation in grace. It brings about filial adoption so that men become Christ's brethren, as Jesus himself called his disciples after his Resurrection: "Go and tell my brethren." We are brethren not by nature, but by the gift of grace, because that adoptive filiation gains us a real share in the life of the only Son, which was fully revealed in his Resurrection.

655 Finally, Christ's Resurrection—and the risen Christ himself—is the principle and source of our future resurrection: "Christ has been raised from the dead, the first fruits of those who have fallen asleep. . . For as in Adam all die, so also in Christ shall all be made alive." The risen Christ lives in the hearts of his faithful while they await that fulfillment. In Christ, Christians "have tasted. . . the powers of the age to come" and their lives are swept up by Christ into the heart of divine life, so that they may "live no longer for themselves but for him who for their sake died and was raised." [29]

Surprised by Hope: Rethinking Heaven, the Resurrection, and the Mission of the Church, N.T. Wright

"The Strange Story of Easter"

There are many smaller arguments which might be brought in at this point, but which we can only summarize. To begin with, the other proposals that are regularly advanced as rival explanations to the early Christian one:

1 Jesus didn't really die; someone gave him a drug which made him look like dead, and he revived in the tomb. Answer: Roman soldiers knew how to kill people, and no disciple would have been fooled by a half-drugged, beat-up Jesus into thinking he'd defeated death and inaugurated the kingdom.

2 When the women went to the tomb they met someone else (perhaps James, Jesus' brother, who looked like him), and in the half-light they thought it was Jesus himself.

Answer: they would have noticed soon enough.

3 Jesus only appeared to people who believed in him. Answer: the accounts make it clear that Thomas and Paul do not come into this category; and actually none of Jesus' followers believed, after his death, that he really was the Messiah, let alone that he was in any sense divine.

4 The accounts we have are biased. Answer: so is all history, all journalism. Every photo is taken by somebody from some angle.

5 They began by saying "he will be raised" as people had done of the martyrs, and this quickly passed into saying "he has been raised" which was functionally equivalent. Answer: no, it wasn't.

6 Lots of people have visions of someone they love who has just died; this was what happened to the disciples. Answer: they knew perfectly well about things like that, and they had language for it; they would say "it's his angel" or "it's his spirit" or "his ghost." They wouldn't say "he's been raised from the dead."

7 Perhaps the most popular: what actually happened was that they had some kind of rich "spiritual" experience, which they interpreted through Jewish categories. Jesus after all really was alive, spiritually, and they were still in touch with him. Answer: that is simply a description of a noble death followed by a Platonic immortality. Resurrection was and is the defeat of death, not simply a nicer description of it; and it's something that happens some while after the moment of death, not immediately.

Equally, we may just notice three of the numerous small-scale arguments which are often, and quite rightly, advanced to support the belief that Jesus did indeed rise from the dead:

1 Jewish tombs, especially those of martyrs, were venerated and often became shrines. There is no sign whatever of that having happened with Jesus' grave.

2 The early church's emphasis on the first day of the week as their special day is very hard to explain unless something striking really did happen then. A gradual or even sudden dawning of faith is hardly sufficient to explain it.

3 The disciples were hardly likely to go out and suffer and die for a belief that wasn't firmly anchored in fact. This is an important point, though subject to the weakness that they might have been genuinely mistaken: they believed the resurrection of Jesus to be a fact, and acted on that belief, but we know (so it would be said) that they were wrong. All this brings us face to face with the ultimate question. The empty tomb and the meetings with Jesus are as well established, by the arguments I have advanced, as any historical data could expect to be. They are, in combination, the only possible explanation for the stories and beliefs that grew up so quickly among Jesus' followers.

How, in turn, do we explain them?

In any other historical enquiry, the answer would be so obvious that it would hardly need saying. Here, of course, this obvious answer ("well, it actually happened") is so shocking, so earth-shattering, that we rightly pause before leaping into the unknown. And here, indeed, as some skeptical friends have cheerfully pointed out to me, it is always possible for anyone to follow the argument so far and to say, simply, "I don't have a good explanation for what happened to cause the empty tomb and the appearances, but I choose to maintain my belief that dead people don't rise and therefore conclude that something else must have happened, even though we can't tell what it was." That is fine; I respect that position; but I simply note that it is indeed then a matter of choice, not a matter of saying that something called "scientific historiography" itself forces us to take that route. [30]

SUGGESTED READING

Wright, N. T. *The Resurrection of the Son of God,* 2003.

27. St. John Chrysostom, "The Easter Sermon of John Chrysostom."
28. Col. 1:13-14 NASB.
29. Catechism of the Catholic Church 651-655: "The Meaning and Saving Significance of the Resurrection", 170-171.
30. Wright, N.T., *Surprised by Hope,* 72-73.

Chapter Seven

Words Are Not Enough

"It is the Holy Spirit, therefore, who instills the sentiment of divine sonship into the heart, who makes us feel (not just know!) that we are children of God. The Spirit himself joins with our spirit to bear witness that we are children of God (Rom. 8:16). This fundamental work of the Holy Spirit sometimes takes places in a sudden and intense way in the life of a person... On the occasion of a retreat ... or on the occasion of prayer for a new releasing of the Spirit the soul is filled with a new light in which God reveals himself in a way as Father. ... A feeling of great trust and confidence and a completely new sense of the condescension of God are experienced. At other times, instead, this revelation of the Father is accompanied by such a strong feeling of God's majesty and transcendence that the soul is overwhelmed." [31]

- Raniero Cantalamessa,
Life in the Lordship of Christ

THE GRACE: *To Be Overwhelmed*

And I will ask the Father, and he will give you another helper [Paraclete], to be with you forever, even the Spirit of truth . . .you know him, for he dwells with you, and will be in you.[32]

John 14:16-17

THEMES

The Holy Spirit...

- Convinces me that Jesus came to rescue me.
- Moves me to surrender.
- Gives me a heart to go rescue others.

---

31. Cantalamessa, *Life in the Lordship of Christ*, 167-168.
32. Jn. 14:16-17 RSV.

QUESTIONS TO CONSIDER

Reflection on the Spirit

- Holy Spirit, help me to know these are not just words.
- Holy Spirit, take me to Calvary.
- Holy Spirit, convince me that Jesus is on the cross for me.
- Holy Spirit, convince me that God is my Father.
- Holy Spirit, convince me that I am his beloved son/daughter.
- Holy Spirit, overwhelm me now.

_____

_____

_____

_____

_____

_____

_____

_____

_____

_____

_____

_____

_____

_____

_____

_____

_____

_____

_____

_____

_____

_____

_____

_____

_____

_____

_____

_____

Facilitator Resources

Chapter Summary

The extraordinary news of the gospel, that we have been rescued from the bondage of Sin, Death, and Satan by God Himself in the person of Jesus, stirs each of us ultimately to ask the question, "How, then, should I respond?" The Catholic Church teaches that there ought to be two types of responses—inward and outward expressions of faith. But by the gift of grace, none of us are left to do either on our own. God has sent the Holy Spirit who provides the strength that enables each of us to entrust our life fully to Jesus Christ.

GOALS

● Understanding how the Holy Spirit empowers our response to God's love and mercy.

● Recognizing what it is God the Father asks of each of us.

Chapter Topics

- Responding to Rescue
- The Role of the Holy Spirit

PASTORAL NOTES

1. Prayer ministry on retreat
A reminder that prayer is the foundation of *The Rescue Project*. Everything we do begins and ends with prayer throughout the weekly experience. On the retreat, the group facilitators move into praying with and for their participants individually for an outpouring of the Holy Spirit to be convinced that all God has done is for them, personally, by name and to surrender to Jesus. While everyone is invited to prayer ministry, no one should be forced or compelled to receive it.

2. The emotion of retreat
As a facilitator, you may find yourself playing a number of roles while on retreat with your group. Some participants may want to talk individually with you and ask follow-up questions to ideas presented during the experience. Others may want to share with you what they are thinking and feeling–both good and bad. Understand

that retreats can be emotional experiences for many, so be ready and rely on all the things that make good group leaders: always be attentive, listen, and do your best to make participants feel safe, cared for, and loved.

QUESTIONS TO CONSIDER

Reflection on the Spirit
Rather than guide a discussion here, encourage participants not only to reflect personally on each of these questions but also to use the space provided in their guides when they are moved to do so. Again, reassure participants that they will not be required to share anything aloud.

Holy Spirit,
help me to know these are not just words.

Holy Spirit, take me to Calvary.

Holy Spirit,
convince me that Jesus is on the cross for me.

Holy Spirit,
convince me that God is my Father.

Holy Spirit,
convince me that
I am His beloved son/daughter.

Holy Spirit, overwhelm me now.

Chapter Eight

What Does He Want from Me?

"...when the Son of Man comes, will he find faith on earth?"

Luke 18:8

THE GRACE: *To Be Overwhelmed*

...God is love.
1 John 4:8

THEMES

What Is Faith?

Faith is *not*:
- *A feeling*
- *Blind*
- *Intellectual assent*

Faith *is*:
- *God's work in me to which I respond*
- *A way of knowing*
- *Surrender*

How Do I Surrender?

- The easier part: *Clinging to the Lord who rescued you*
- The harder, more challenging part: *Detaching from your idols*

QUESTIONS TO CONSIDER

- What are the idols in my life?
- What would detaching from the idols in my life look like practically?

_____

_____

_____

_____

_____

_____

_____

_____

_____

Facilitator Resources

Created | Captured | Rescued | Response

Chapter Summary

The inward expression of faith God calls for from each of us culminates with our complete surrendering to Him—heart, soul, strength, and mind. But what does that actually look like? It begins with worship, truly giving God the honor, reverence, and devotion He is due; it entails detaching from our idols, the things of this world that absorb our hearts and minds more than God; it involves giving Him praise and thanks, most especially through regular prayer and participation in the Mass, where God offers to each of us as individuals the most fundamental expression of love—union with Himself in the Eucharist.

GOALS

- Recognizing the necessity of worship, thanksgiving, and surrender.
- Understanding the true role of the Mass in our lives.

Chapter Topics

- Our Personal Response to Jesus
- God's Preferred Way of Being Thanked

PASTORAL NOTES

Rather than guide a discussion here, encourage participants not only to reflect personally on these questions but also to write out their responses in the space provided in their guides. Again, reassure participants that they will not be required to share anything aloud.

What are the idols in your life?

What would detaching from the idols in your life look like practically?

Prayer of Surrender

Father,

I believe that out of your infinite love you created me. I come before you, just as I am, with all my brokenness, wounds, and hurts. I am sorry for all the times I have believed the enemy's lies that you are not a good Father and don't love me. I repent and ask you to forgive me for all of my sins.

Jesus,
Thank you for coming to rescue me from Sin, Death, Hell, and Satan. I surrender to you right now and invite you to be Lord over every area of my entire life.

Come, Holy Spirit,
Flood my soul with the love of the Father and convince me that I matter, I'm worth the trouble, and that in God's eyes I'm worth dying for.

Come, Holy Spirit...

I **thirst** for you

It is true.

I stand at the door of your heart, day and night. Even when you are not listening, even when you doubt it could be me, I am there: waiting for even the smallest signal of your response, even the smallest suggestion of an invitation that will permit me to enter.

And I want you to know that each time you invite me, I do come always, without fail. Silent and invisible I come, yet with a power and a love most infinite, bringing the many gifts of my Spirit. I come with my mercy, with my desire to forgive and heal you, with a love for you that goes beyond your comprehension—a love every bit as great as the love I have received from the Father. I come, longing to console you and give you strength, to lift you up and bind all your wounds. I bring you my light, to dispel your darkness and all your doubts. I come with my power, that I might carry you and all your burdens; with my grace, to touch your heart and transform your life; and my peace, to still your soul.

I know you like the palm of my hand. I know everything about you. Even the hairs of your head I have counted. Nothing in your life is unimportant to me. I have followed you through the years and I have always loved you even when you have strayed. I know every one of your problems. I know your needs and your worries and yes, I know all your sins.

But I tell you again that I love you, not for what you have or ceased to do, I love you for you, for the beauty and the dignity my Father gave you by creating you in his own image. It is a dignity you have often forgotten, a beauty you have tarnished by sin. But I love you as you are, and I have shed my blood to rescue you. If you only ask me with faith. My grace will touch all that needs changing in your life: I will give you the strength to free yourself from sin and from all its destructive power.

I know what is in your heart; I know your loneliness and all your wounds; the rejections, the judgments, the humiliations. I carried it all before you. And I carried it all for you, so you could share my strength and my victory. I know especially your need for love—how much you are thirsting to be loved and cherished. But how often you have thirsted in vain, by seeking that love selfishly, striving to fill the emptiness inside you with passing pleasures-with even the greater emptiness of sin. Do you thirst for love? "Come to me all who thirst..." (John 7:37). I will satisfy you and fill you. Do you thirst to be loved?

I love you more than you can imagine-to the point of dying on a cross for you.

I thirst for you. Yes, that is the only way to even begin to describe my love for you.

I thirst for you. That is the only way to even begin to describe my love for you. I thirst for you. I thirst to love you and to be loved by you; that is how precious you are to me. I thirst for you. Come to me, and I will fill your heart and heal your wounds. I will make you a new creation and give you peace even in your trials. I thirst for you.

You must never doubt my mercy, my acceptance of you, my desire to forgive, my longing to bless you and live my life in you. I thirst for you. If you feel unimportant in the eyes of the world, that matters not at all. For me, there is no one more important in the world than you. I thirst for you. Open to me, come to me, thirst for me, give me your life, and I will prove to you how important you are for my heart.

Don't you realize that my Father already has a perfect plan to transform your life, beginning from this moment? Trust in me. Ask me every day to enter and take charge of your life, and I will. I promise you before my Father in Heaven that I will work miracles in your life.

Why would I do this? Because I thirst for you. All I ask of you is that you entrust yourself completely to me. I will do all the rest.

Even now, I behold the place my Father has prepared for you in my kingdom. Remember that you are a pilgrim in this life, on a journey home. Sin can never satisfy you, or bring the peace you seek. All that you have sought outside of me has only left you more empty, so do not cling to the things of this life. Above all, do not run from me when you fall. Come to me without delay. When you give me your sins, you give me the joy of being your Savior. There is nothing I cannot forgive and heal; so come now, and unburden your soul.

No matter how far you may wander, no matter how often you forget me, no matter how many crosses you bear in this life; there is one thing I want you to always remember, one thing that will never change: I thirst for you–just as you are. You don't need to change to believe in my love, for it will be your belief in my love that will change you. You forget me, and yet I am seeking you every moment of the day–standing before the doors of your heart and knocking. Do you find this hard to believe?

Then look again at the cross, look at my heart that was pierced for you. Have you not understood my cross? Then listen again to the words I spoke there, for they tell you clearly why I endured all this for you: "I thirst..." *(John 19: 28)*. Yes, I thirst for you. I have never stopped seeking to love you and be loved by you. You have tried many other things in your search for happiness; why not try opening up your heart to me, right now, more than you ever have before? And when you finally open the door of your heart, whenever you come close enough, you will then hear me say to you again and again, not in mere human words but in spirit: No matter what you have done, I love you for your own sake. So come to me with your misery and your sins, with your troubles and needs, and with all your longing to be loved–because I stand at the door of your heart and knock.

Open up to me, for I thirst for you. [33]

- St. Mother Teresa of Calcutta

SUGGESTED READING

Driscoll, Fr. Jeremy. *Awesome Glory: Resurrection in Scripture, Liturgy, and Theology,* 2019.

Driscoll, Fr. Jeremy. *What Happens at Mass,* 2005.

Hahn, Dr. Scott. *The Lamb's Supper: The Mass as Heaven on Earth,* 1999.

33. St. Mother Teresa, "I Thirst for You."

Chapter Nine

Getting Clarity on the Mission

"In the high-stakes drama all around us, we have each been given a part to play, one that bears our name and no one else's. We each have the mercy of God to receive, a self to put to death, a Kingdom to gain, a battle to fight and spiritual enemies to slay, comrades to aid, rebels to win over. ... The ancient battle rages all around us, and the adventure we were born for beckons." [34]

- Sophia Consulting,
The Christian Cosmic Narrative

THE GRACE: *Magnanimity*

You are the light of the world ... people [do not] light a lamp and put it under a basket, but on a stand, and it gives light to all in the house.

Matthew 5:14-15

THEMES

The Mission

1. **Sabotage and Resistance**

_____

_____

_____

_____

_____

_____

2. Reconciliation

_____

_____

_____

_____

_____

_____

3. Re-creation

_____

_____

_____

_____

_____

_____

4. Healing

_____

_____

_____

5. Restoration

_____

_____

_____

_____

_____

6. Ambassadorship

_____

_____

_____

_____

_____

_____

34. Sophia Consulting, *The Christian Cosmic Narrative*, 156.

QUESTIONS TO CONSIDER

- Please read the reflection *"Two other essential missions: Prayer and Suffering"* below. What resonates with me and why?
- Has my understanding of the mission of the disciple changed? How and why?
- Which mission(s) speaks the most to me? Why?

As we conclude this chapter, prayerfully discern how God may be inviting you now to write the next chapter of His-story.

_____

_____

_____

_____

_____

_____

_____

_____

Two other essential missions:
Prayer and Suffering

Any attempt to give an exhaustive description of the mission that Jesus sends us in order to accomplish will certainly fall short. In this talk, we have called attention to six missions, if you will, that the Lord calls us to carry out: resistance, reconciliation, re-creation, healing, transformation, and ambassadors.

There are, however, two additional missions that must be mentioned as we close: prayer and suffering.

First, prayer. It is crucial to remember that baptism *really* does something in a person. For example, It really washes away sin; transfers us from the dominion and reign of darkness into the kingdom of God's beloved Son; makes us new creatures; causes us to become temples of the Holy Spirit; incorporates us into the Body of Christ; makes us adopted sons and daughters of God and more besides (cf. Acts 2:38; 22:16; Col. 1:13-14; Rom. 8:14-17;12:4-5; 1 Cor. 6:19; 12:12-14; 2 Cor. 5:17; *The Catechism of the Catholic Church* nos. 1262-1274).

Baptism, though, also makes a person a priest, or, more precisely, to share in Jesus' own priesthood. This is commonly referred to as "the priesthood of all believers," as distinct from the ministerial priesthood. Saint Peter reminds the early Christian community that they are "a chosen race, a royal *priesthood*" (1 Peter 2:5). Peter is talking to all of the people, men and women, who have been reborn in baptism. The seer in Revelation writes, "To him who loves us and has freed us from our sins by his blood and made us a kingdom, priests to his God and Father" (Rev. 1:5-6). Likewise, the seer is referring to *everyone* born anew of water and the Holy Spirit.

What do priests *do*? Abbott Jeremy Driscoll says, "It is the priest's work to bring another before God in prayer." We can do this because we have access to God. *This is amazing!* If you tried to walk into the White House to meet the President you would certainly be turned away, and perhaps arrested! If you tried to walk into your doctor's office without an appointment, more than likely you would be told that you have to call and schedule a visit. If you walked in and tried to see the CEO of virtually any organization, you would probably be told it's simply not possible.

But we can talk to God...anytime!

And this is an essential part of our mission as disciples of Jesus. We are all called to stand, sit, kneel, or lie prostrate in agonizing prayer for the world, our spouse, our children, co workers, friends, leaders—everyone and anyone. We are called to lift them up to the One who is Love and desires all men and women to be saved (cf. 1 Tim. 2:4). We are allowed, invited even, to pound on the Sacred Heart of Jesus, the One who has rescued us from Sin, Death, Satan, and Hell.

Priests, however, also offer sacrifices, and this is a second mission we are all sent by Jesus in order to accomplish.

Saint Paul, in his Letter to the Romans, exhorts Christians this way: "Present your bodies as a living sacrifice, holy and acceptable to God, which is your spiritual worship" (Rom. 12:2).

The imagery Paul is drawing on here is rather humorous, even if painful. Sacrifices in his day were usually animals placed by a priest atop an altar to be slain and burned up as an offering to the Roman gods and goddesses. This was done in an attempt to either win the favor of the gods or to appease their wrath. Paul is telling us that we are called to place ourselves on the altar, not to win God's favor or appease him, but out of gratitude for all He has already done for us and so that we can become holy (the literal meaning of sacrifice). A key difference, however, is that we are *living* sacrifices, which means the body keeps crawling off the altar! Each day we have to choose to crawl back on, in gratitude and trusting in our Father's great love made manifest in Jesus.

But is there more to this call to offer ourselves as a sacrifice than meets the eye at first glance?

One of the more challenging verses in all of the Bible is Colossians 1:24. Saint Paul says, "I fill up in my flesh what is lacking in the sufferings of Christ for the sake of his body, which is the Church." What in the world is "lacking" in the sufferings of Christ? Does Paul mean to convey that what Jesus did in going to war to rescue us was close but not quite enough to accomplish all that He came to do? Hardly. The only thing "lacking" in Jesus' suffering is our participation in it.

Now, it must be stated right away, there are two distinct kinds of suffering. On the one hand, there are sufferings we might take on voluntarily, like fasting or some other act of penance; and, on the other hand, there are involuntary sufferings that come to us, like chronic pain or cancer.

As disciples of Jesus we are sent in order to unite our suffering to the cross of Jesus for the sake of the world. This is immensely important since, with regards to involuntary suffering, it's not a question of *if* it's going to come to us in this life, only *how* and *when*.

The narrative of the culture at large sees suffering as a waste, of no value whatsoever. Men and women in nursing homes and hospitals, or confined to their own homes, or wherever pain may find them, can be strongly tempted to think that what they are going through has no point, is of no value, and is in vain.

The disciple of Jesus knows a different story. If we had been there on that day we now call "Good Friday," and seen Jesus on the cross between the two thieves, we would certainly have thought to ourselves, "What an utter waste." We would have thought that nothing good would come from that.

And we would have been wrong.

Disciples of Jesus understand that he rescued us precisely by his suffering on the cross, wherein he revealed to us the Father's love, made atonement for our sins, and went to war to defeat the powers of Sin, Death, and Satan.

Disciples of Jesus likewise understand that Jesus didn't promise us that if we believed in him he would protect us from any and all suffering. Instead, the New Testament is filled with passages on how we will suffer with and for Jesus before we enter fully into his kingdom (cf. among so many verses Mark 8:34; Rom. 8:17; Phil. 1:29; 1 Pet. 4:12-16).

However, as it was with Jesus on the cross, so it is with us when we suffer.

It is not a waste, or in vain, or at least it need not be. When we suffer we can use it. And God can do great things through it.

It was once common to hear someone encourage another who was suffering to "offer it up." That can strike us, perhaps, as being a bit passive. Some have found it more helpful, remembering Paul's words in Col. 1:24, to actively unite what they're going through—chemotherapy, a migraine, chronic back pain, depression, or any other way that suffering comes to us—to the cross of Jesus, trusting that one day they will understand how God used this. The important thing is to understand that nothing we are enduring right now, no matter how painful it may be, need be in vain!

An example of prayer and suffering:

Let me end by offering one final example, one of both prayer and suffering. I mentioned in the video how Jesus used my father as an instrument of healing in my mother's life, so much so that she said to him as he lay in his casket, "Honey, because of you I know who God is." Jesus likewise used my mother as an example of prayer and suffering.

My mom spent most of the last years of her life in intense, chronic pain. Pain is usually measured on a scale of 1-10. Many days her pain was something like a 15. My mother, however, when she was younger, had experienced a miraculous healing, something right out of the pages of the Gospels or The Acts of the Apostles. The point in mentioning that is to say she knew firsthand God's power and that miracles were not confined to the past. She came to understand over time, however, that the same Lord who had once healed her was now inviting her to do the very thing Paul did in his life so many years before: to fill up in her own flesh what was lacking in the sufferings of Christ for the sake of others.

And, so, my mom, without in any way ever romanticizing pain, learned to pray in a new way, learned to crawl atop the altar out of love for the sake of others. When I asked her about this once, she told me that she said to the Lord, "Jesus, you know that I do not want this pain and that I so want you to release me from it. But I trust that this is not in vain, is not useless, is not meaningless–anymore than your cross was. And, so, I unite this to your cross for..." and then she got the idea to start writing down names of people who were in need. At first it was just a few–my dad, her children, her grandchildren and great grandchildren. Over time, however, the lists grew. She started to keep a ledger of prayer intentions on legal pads beside the hospital bed where she lay most of the day, or on the kitchen counter around which she would walk to ease the pain. It might be a couple she heard was having marital difficulties. A young man who was suicidal and battling depression. A girl who was pregnant and considering an abortion. Leaders of nations. People discerning huge decisions. It was overwhelming to see how many names–and how many legal pads!–there were. Gradually, people began to hear about this. They would ask me, or my siblings, to please ask my mom to write their name, or the name of a loved one, in her legal pads.

When my mom finally died and her pain was over, I had an image of Jesus walking with her, taking her on a sort of tour.

As they walked, He started to show her various homes and they were able to look inside the homes and see the people inside. That couple who had been struggling in their marriage and had managed to stay the course. The young man who had persevered through the depression. The young girl and the child she had chosen to keep. On and on they walked together, and after each house,

Jesus simply smiled at my mother and said to her, "It was by my grace that they were able to do those things. But it was your participation in my cross that made it possible. Well done, good and faithful servant!"

To all of you, then, in pain right now, suffering in mind, body, or spirit, please know how valuable, how immensely valuable, you are! You are the spiritual backbone of those who are out there serving as agents of resistance, reconciliation, re-creation, healing, transformation, and ambassadors. Stay strong! Keep the faith! We desperately need you!

Facilitator Resources

Chapter Summary

The outward expression of faith God calls for from each of us is to participate as active agents in the liberation and transformation of His world. The message of Easter is that Jesus has inaugurated the recreation of all things through his dying and rising, and we, collectively and as individuals, are commissioned to partake in the building of His kingdom—right here and right now—through our marriages, families, and friendships; in our homes, communities, and cultural institutions; and as part of our work as professionals, citizens, and people of faith.

GOALS

- Recognizing that the Easter proclamation calls us to Christian action in this life.

- Understanding our mission as people who have been rescued.

Chapter Topics

- Building God's Kingdom

- Becoming Agents of Transformation

PASTORAL NOTES

Magnanimity: An Explanation

Magnanimity literally means to have a great soul. St. Aquinas describes it as a stretching forth of the mind to great things and considers it as belonging to the virtue of fortitude or courage. The Angelic Doctor adds that this virtue makes a man deem himself worthy of great things in consideration of the gifts he holds from God.

The final chapter of The Rescue Project puts forth a number of examples and heroes who understood that they were destined by God to live in their particular time. Each of them lived and acted in such a way that they sought to continue the mission Jesus began on Easter Sunday. Each of them is a model of magnanimity. So, too, is our patroness, Joan of Arc. In fact, it would be hard to find a single saint that didn't demonstrate this virtue.

The Mission
With each of these categories, invite participants to imagine ways that they might become this particular type of agent of transformation in the world.

1. Sabotage and Resistance

2. Reconciliation

3. Re-Creation

4. Healing

5. Restoration

6. Ambassadorship

QUESTIONS TO CONSIDER

What resonates with you and why?
Prayer and suffering can often be misunderstood by Christians. On the one hand, prayer is something that many of us think of as largely personal (something we do quietly and alone) and inwardly focused (what do I

need, what am I concerned with). And on the other hand, suffering is something that most people spend huge amounts of time avoiding—at least the involuntary kind of suffering (pain, illness). But the Church invites us to see these two experiences—prayer and suffering—as part of our mission as disciples of Jesus. The more we consider prayer as an opportunity to unite ourselves to others by lifting our friends, families, neighbors, even strangers up to the Lord, the more we are able to participate in the mystical body of Christ. The same goes for suffering. Both kinds of suffering—voluntary and involuntary—are opportunities to go on mission for the Church. Whether we're fasting or enduring some sort of great pain, we can unite it to Jesus's suffering on the cross and then ask God can do great things with it. Working in service to our brothers and sisters in Christ is the definition of being on mission, and both prayer and suffering allow us to do just that!

Has your understanding of the mission of the disciple changed? How and why?
It is not uncommon for Catholics to view getting to mass each week and receiving the sacraments as the sum total of what is expected of us as Christians. But there is so much more. Ask participants to share how their understanding of the faith may have been transformed by *The Rescue Project*, particularly chapter 9. As much as you're able, encourage them to imagine what the next set of days, weeks, months look like for them personally as a result of their new appreciation for what it means to be a disciple of Jesus.

Which mission(s) speaks the most to you? Why?
Be sure to include not just the six categories discussed in the video for chapter 9 (sabotage and resistance, reconciliation, re-creation, healing, restoration, and ambassadorship) but also the two missions of prayer and suffering mentioned in *The Rescue Project Story Guide*. Feel free to bring into this conversation the reflection at the end chapter 9 in the Story Guide ("prayerfully discern how God may be inviting you now to write the next chapter of His-story").

DEEPER QUESTIONS

1. Have you ever considered that, like St. Joan of Arc, you were born for this historical moment and a specific mission? What do you think that might be?

2. The parable of "The Good Samaritan" teaches us that in order to be equipped for mission as a Christian disciple, we need to conform our hearts to the heart of Jesus. What are some of the ways that happens?

3. Has your understanding of The Great Commission ("Go therefore and make disciples of all nations" [Matthew 28:19]) changed at all in light of the idea that "rescued people rescue people"? How?

"I am not afraid. God is with me.
I was born for this."
- *St. Joan of Arc*

Know The Story

Rescued People
Rescue **People**

Bibliography

Baptismal Ritual of the Catholic Church, 158.

Cantalamessa, Raniero. *Life in the Lordship of Christ:* A spiritual commentary on the letter to the Romans. London: Darton, Longman and Todd, 1992.

"The Mystery of Creation"; "The Fall of the Angels"; "Original Sin"; and "The Meaning and Saving Significance of the Resurrection" in the *Catechism of the Catholic Church,* 2nd ed., for the United States of America. Vatican: Libreria Editrice Vaticana, 1994.

The Council of Chalcedon. "The Letter of Pope Leo to Flavian."

Hahn, Dr. Scott. *Commentary on Roman.* Grand Rapids, MI: Baker Academic, a division of Baker Publishing Group, 2017.

Kreeft, Peter. *The Greatest Philosopher Who Ever Lived.* San Francisco, CA: Ignatius Press, 2021.

Knoebel, Thomas L. (quoting Isidore of Seville). "De Ecclesiasticis Officiis, 14.13" in *Sententiae.* Paulist Press, 2008.

Lectionary for Mass. Chicago, IL: Liturgy Training Publications, 2002.

Maximus the Confessor. *Mystery of the Divine Incarnation.*

"The Order of Baptism of Children," English Translation according to the Second Typical Edition. Collegeville, MN: Liturgical Press, 2019.

Ratzinger, Joseph. *Credo for Today: What Christians Believe.* San Francisco, CA: Ignatius Press, 2009.

Sheed, Frank. *To Know Christ Jesus.* San Francisco, CA: Ignatius Press, 2012.

Sophia Consulting. *The Christian Cosmic Narrative, The Deep History of the World*. Detroit, MI: ACTS XXIX Press, 2021.

St. Augustine. "Expositions of the Psalms 51-72 (J.E. Rotelle, Ed.) Vol 17." Hyde Park, New York: New City Press, 2001.

St. Bernard. "The Fountains of the Savior" in *Sermons on Advent & Christmas*. London: Benziger Bros, 1909.

St. Bonaventure. The Soul's Journey to God: The Tree of Life: The Life of St. Francis. Mahwah, NJ: Paulist Press, 1978.

St. Ephrem the Syrian. "A Sermon on the Cross of Christ."

St. Gregory of Nyssa. "Sermon on the Ascension" (chapter XXIV) in *The Great Catechism*.

St. Ignatius of Antioch. "The Second Epistle of Ignatius to the Ephesians, Vol. 1". Buffalo, NY: Christian Literature Company, 1885.

St. Irenaeus. *The Demonstration of the Apostolic Preaching*.

St. John Chrysostom. "The Easter Sermon of John Chrysostom, Pastor of Constantinople."

St. Justin Martyr. "Dialogue with Trypho, (A.D. 155)."

St. Melito of Sardis. "Sermon on The Passover."

St. Mother Teresa of Calcutta. "I Thirst for You."

Wright, N.T. *Surprised by Hope: Rethinking Heaven, the Resurrection, and the Mission of the Church*. HarperOne, an imprint of HarperCollins Publishers, 2018.

Wright, N.T. *Jesus and the Victory of God*. London: SPCK, 2015.